Are you worried you about to **burn out?**

This book is for you if...

- Your work is going crazy and you want to protect your wellbeing.
- You find yourself working longer and longer hours just to keep on top of everything.
- You're aspirational, competitive and driven to succeed.
- You don't seem able to get the results you used to get.
- You feel exhausted all the time.
- You feel you're always having to push yourself.
- You have high standards and believe everything in life has to be perfect.
- Your 'get up and go' has got up and gone.
- You're struggling to cope with the demands and pressures of life.
- You crave sweet foods – anything that gives you a quick fix of energy.
- You need copious amounts of coffee to get you through the day and alcohol to calm you down in the evening.
- You have trouble getting to sleep or staying asleep.
- You've become uncharacteristically grumpy or irritable.
- You feel wired but exhausted.
- You find it difficult to say no to people – even when you're overwhelmed with work.
- You can be very critical of yourself.
- You haven't got the energy to exercise and when you do, it wipes you out.
- You are putting weight on around your middle yet you don't think you eat very much.
- You're forgetful and find it difficult to concentrate.
- You seem to be more anxious about things than you've ever been before.
- You have no time for a social life.

What people are saying about Susan

Susan brings her substantial professional expertise to the physical and mental strains which feel increasingly common in modern life, with a welcome focus on practical advice and support for young people making their way in the world.
Rt Hon Jeremy Hunt MP

I have read this excellent book as a mother of young professionals and an employer of young professionals and have found it invaluable. It is extremely readable, insightful and most importantly inspires the reader with compelling evidence at a physical and emotional level. It does so in a most inspiring and helpful way that encourages the reader to own their own fate. This is a book for "you". As an experienced professional I wish I had access to this earlier in my career but now it has been valuable as a tool for me in understanding the challenges to wellbeing we all face today. This is a great book for personal resilience for individuals and employers alike. A must read.
Nicky Murdoch MBE, CEO The St John & Red Cross Defence Medical Welfare Service (DMWS)

Susan Scott has provided Young Professionals with another excellent guide. This time it's on how to prevent burnout and reignite your life and career. Burnout is notoriously difficult to identify with signs and symptoms sometimes indistinguishable from depression. Both conditions are potentially very dangerous to our health and wellbeing, so avoiding burnout is vitally important for a happy and successful professional and personal life. This guide beautifully balances the nutritional and psychological aspects of burnout, how it impacts on us and how to prevent burnout from occurring in the first place. There is a thorough explanation of what happens to our bodies under stressful conditions, and how various glands and hormones act to protect us. When these are overloaded we find ourselves experiencing sensations that interfere with our energy, concentration and our performance. There is an equally thorough explanation of how our brains respond under stressful conditions, and the function of parts of our brain in safeguarding our health. When these are overloaded for any length of time, the consequences can be dire. The explanations lead into a series of self-help methods of assessing how we are currently functioning, whether we are close to burnout, and what to do about it. The assessments cover both the nutritional and psychological aspects of our bodies, and highlights the danger signals in both how we eat and sleep as well as the personalities that might disadvantage our health and wellbeing. The advice and guidance is superb about how we benefit from different foods and supplements, ways of preparing ourselves for sleep, and approaches to maintaining our psychological health and wellbeing, particularly at work. Every suggestion has a solid and well argued reason for adoption, and all of the advice makes absolute sense. The challenge, as always for the reader, is to be sufficiently disciplined to take the advice and guidance and build them into the daily life of a Young Professional.

Dr Derek Mowbray BA MS MSc(Econ) PhD DipPsych CPsychol CSci FBPsS FIHM FISMA. CEO The Wellbeing and Performance Group

I was having real trouble taking on too much at work and never saying no. I knew a restructure was coming up and I was desperate to show senior management how needed I was for the organisation. It all came to a head during a particularly busy period. I had been running on adrenaline for so long and almost suddenly it all ran out. I felt exhausted and like I couldn't take one more thing on. I spoke to Susan and she really helped me. Susan has an amazing style of being direct but also incredibly supportive. She coached me to understand what was happening and how to take back control again.

Manager, Charity Sector

I was managing a difficult project with a difficult manager with a lot of big stressful events happening at the same time in my personal life. I ended up burning out which really affected me emotionally. Susan supported me and helped me with the coping mechanisms to recover. I now understand the triggers better and how to cope better. Susan's experience and knowledge means that she understands what's happening physically and mentally when you're stressed. I'm sure it was this combination that helped me recover much faster.

Manager, Financial Services

*To Jon Lassiter – who insisted I write a book about burnout.
Thank you for your cajoling!*

About Susan Scott
MSc, FCIPD, FISMA, MABP, MBANT

Susan is a business psychologist, a nutritional therapist, a trainer, a consultant and a coach, as well as a public speaker and the author of the best-selling book, "How to have an outstanding career".

She has worked extensively in the Information Technology, Management Consultancy, Finance, Legal and Charity sectors and has designed and delivered major change management projects and management, leadership and wellbeing programmes for numerous private and public sector organisations across the UK, Europe, USA and Australasia. In tandem with consulting work, Susan ran a nutritional therapy clinic for executives experiencing burnout.

Susan brings a blended mind and body approach to her work. She believes passionately that everyone, but in particular, the Young Professional, deserves to work in ways that foster their resilience, performance and career. And because of her extensive experience working within organisations, she is very aware of the drive and passion that Young Professionals bring to their work and why this needs to be managed in ways that do not lead them down the road to burnout.

Susan has an MSc in Organisational Behaviour from the University of London, a Diploma in Nutritional Therapy (Distinction) from the Institute for Optimum Nutrition and is registered with The Nutritional Therapy Council.

She is a Fellow of the Chartered Institute of Personnel and Development and a Fellow of the International Stress Management Association. She is also a Principal Member of the Association for Business Psychology and a Member of the British Association of Applied Nutrition and Nutritional Therapy.

She is a past Chair of the Trustees of the International Stress Management Association (ISMA[UK]) and is the co-author of "The Manager's Role in Stress Prevention."

Learn more

This book is just the beginning of your journey to managing stress and optimising the health of your mind and body.

Learn more about how you can test for adrenal fatigue, download Tips Leaflets for free and keep up to date with more insights by visiting my website **www.youngprofs.net**

HOW TO PREVENT BURNOUT

and reignite your life and career

To Gary

Remembering happy times
in South America,

Susan

x

SUSAN SCOTT

Published by
Filament Publishing Ltd
16 Croydon Road, Beddington, Croydon,
Surrey, CR0 4PA, United Kingdom.
Telephone +44 (0)20 8688 2598
www.filamentpublishing.com

ISBN 978-1-912256-36-5

Printed by IngramSpark.

Contents

Acknowledgements

I would like to thank a number of people for their inspiration and support with this book.

My fabulous family who have been there for me all the way along this journey.

Anne Perret, who encouraged me and built up my confidence to do this.

My publisher, Chris Day, from Filament Publishing, who believed in me and my book – even if I had to write another book before publishing this one!

My editor, Liz Sheppard-Jones, from Filament Publishing, whose energy and enthusiasm for the topic made the process so much more exciting.

My designer, Clare Clarke, from Fusion3media, for turning 'words' into an art piece. Incredible talent.

Everyone, over the years and across the world, I have come into contact with in a work setting, in my clinic or even chatted with. All I know, I've learnt from you.

To each of you, thank you

"Learn to stop and you will learn stability,
once stable, you will learn to rest,
in rest, you will learn serenity,
in serenity, you will learn to reflect,
and through reflection, you will succeed."
Tseng-tzu

1: Introduction

- Are you struggling to cope with the demands and pressures of your working life?

- Are you exhausted but feel you just have to keep going to be successful?

- Do you find it hard to sleep as well as you used to?

- Do you rely on caffeine and sweet foods to give you the energy to keep going?

- Are you worried that work may be having a detrimental effect on your health and wellbeing?

- Do you feel your life is out of control?

- Do you sometimes wonder how you can achieve what you want to achieve without crashing and burning in the process?

Yes? Well – you're not alone.

As a Young Professional, you are likely to be focused, highly aspirational and driven to succeed in your career – a career that identifies and defines who you are. But twenty-first century living is tough and getting tougher. I know from the research I have done that Young Professionals are struggling to cope. This age group is at higher risk of burning out than any other working age group.

Young Professionals are career-minded people in the early stages of their working lives, typically between the ages of 21 and 32. They are building a reputation based on their knowledge, skills, impact and influence, wanting to be the best that they can be, and achieve their aspirations. But the demands of a 24/7 society and a full-on job, not to mention other responsibilities and commitments, make it physically and mentally difficult.

Young Professionals can push so hard that it takes them beyond their capacity to bounce back and recover. This puts any sense of desired achievement and reward in jeopardy.

Could this be you?

The good news is that it is perfectly possible to keep yourself physically and mentally strong enough to live the way you want to and achieve your goals without burning out. To do this, you need strategies to keep you mentally and physically well, strategies that build your capacity to cope, and strategies to create the framework for you to live a fulfilling and satisfying life.

Why you need this book

If you want to…

- feel you have the capacity to achieve what you want from life without damaging your health
- enjoy life without feeling exhausted
- live a life that reflects who you really are
- feel able to focus, concentrate and deliver to the high standard you know you are capable of
- sleep well and feel energised and motivated

…then this book is for you.

Only you can put things right. If you're going to achieve career success and avoid burning out in the process, now is the time to take action. You cannot afford not to.

By understanding how a highly pressured life affects you physically and mentally, you will realise just how important it is to manage the pressures you face and to build your resilience.

Eat, drink and think success

This book sets out the techniques I have used time and time again in my clinic for executive burnout. These methods are built on academic study, ongoing research and practical application... and even on some personal experiences.

As a business psychologist and nutritional therapist, I will guide you to eat, drink and think in a way that enhances your capacity to cope and gives you the strength to succeed. It's a mind and body approach – because if you are truly going to succeed, you need to address the needs of both.

This plan is designed to empower you to reverse the effects that unrelenting pressure is having on your mind and body, and return you to a state where you feel your best and get the results you strive for.

Adrenals and attitudes

My twin track mind and body approach works with your 'adrenals and attitudes'. It's about looking after your adrenal glands – two tiny but mighty glands that drive the 'fight or flight' response – and enhancing your state of mind to cope with whatever is thrown at you. The result is that you will flourish rather than self-sabotage and wither.

I'll be giving you the knowledge to help you create a new way of life that has the capacity to reward you with the success you so dearly want. It's about moving you from just surviving to thriving, where you take back control and have all the ingredients required to grow and flourish.

This book will show you:

- what burnout actually is
- what your personal stress triggers are
- what stress does to your mind and body and why it leaves you feeling so ghastly
- why you exhibit certain signs and symptoms when the pressure builds up
- how to enhance the health of your adrenal glands by altering your diet and making certain critically important changes to your lifestyle

You'll also learn about the power of the mind and how you could be the cause of your own downfall. Shifting your mindset from self-sabotaging beliefs that drain your energy and enthusiasm to positive thinking is imperative.

Finally, I want to empower you to take control back and optimise your wellbeing. This means you need to know exactly what to do to remain physically and mentally healthy despite everything that's thrown at you.

Don't allow life to derail you – you deserve better. To make these powerful changes, you just need know-how.

This book is packed with explanations, case studies, questionnaires and activities to complete that put you on your own journey of discovery. There's an abundance of tips along the way to provide you with choices on what you could do to prevent yourself burning out. Picking the ones that will work best for you will have a profound effect.

Having your cake and eating it is just a matter of having the right ingredients and a good recipe – and they're all here in this book for you to take and run with. Wake up, read the writing on the wall and put in the effort to make the changes. No one can do it for you. Do this and you will fly…

How to use the book

If you really want to benefit from your purchase, you will need to immerse yourself. Read the book from cover to cover, working your way through it step by step, taking each part in order. That is the best way to understand what the topic is all about (and there is a lot to understand).

As a result of this powerful knowledge, you can build your ultimate action plan to keep you mentally and physically healthy.

Take your time, open up your mind and work in a space that allows you to concentrate and think deeply. Each section of the book has a series of exercises to allow you to reflect on yourself and the stress you are experiencing. You are likely to find some exercises easier than others. If you are struggling with one at any time, do what you can do then leave the book and do something completely different. During that time, your subconscious mind will be whirring away so when you come back you are likely to see things with a clearer perspective.

As each section of the book closes, you will be given the opportunity to reflect on it and write down the things you found interesting, the things that made you stop and think and the things that inspired ideas for action.

This book has it all, but it is down to you how you use it. The more you put in, the more you will get out. Try not to approach this book as a one-off activity, but a work-life journey. This book has the power to guide you through your whole career until the day you retire. The more you use it, the more successful you can be.

This book is a companion to **'How to have an outstanding career and become the person you've always dreamed of being'** which deals with the steps you need to take to achieve your career goals.

I wish you every success. You only have one life – embrace it and live the dream.

Part 1
Burnout

2: What is burnout?

- Do you feel exhausted most of the time?
- Are you losing your passion for work and life?
- Are you finding yourself overwhelmed by even the simplest of tasks?
- Do you struggle to pull yourself together when you wake in the morning?
- Do you often feel tearful and unable to cope?

If the answer to any of these is Yes then it's time to take stock and change, because you may be approaching burnout.

Burnout is a state of emotional, physical and mental exhaustion which leaves you feeling at rock bottom, alone and unable to cope.

Burnout is utterly miserable. It's much more than just feeling tired all the time.

In a state of burnout, you feel hopeless, empty and isolated to the extent that you can lose all interest in life – you just don't have the energy for it.

Your performance is seriously impeded because you struggle to function. This isn't something corrected by having a few nights of good sleep; by the time you feel like this, burnout has become a permanent mental and physical state with major consequences for your health and vitality.

Why does it happen? Because we allow ourselves to get stuck in 'always doing' mode without taking time to recover and rebalance. We're stressed, struggling to deal with the ever-growing demands of both our work and our personal lives. We are always on the go.

Digital technology means we're now accessible 24/7, so the boundaries between work and personal lives become blurred. At the same time, we want it all – a great job, lovely home, fit body, fulfilling hobbies, happy family – and so we drive ourselves constantly to achieve ever more. I call it 'twenty-first century living'.

Although you may feel that your only choice is to go with it, if you don't take better care of yourself, all this pressure increases your susceptibility to burnout.

Burnout can happen to the best

Burnout doesn't happen overnight. It can take months or even years until eventually, one day, the mind and body says, "enough is enough – you've worn yourself out". If you've let things get this far, then it can take anything from three months to two years to get you up and functioning well again.

The most vulnerable people are those who are also the most highly motivated and dedicated: people who strive to complete everything to the highest standard, those for whom work is their life and for whom it provides the very meaning of their existence.

But you can do something about it. You can prevent it happening in the first place, even if you're reading this and feel you're sliding uncontrollably towards burnout. With a few changes to your diet, lifestyle and thinking patterns you can not only prevent it, but find yourself feeling energised, focused and performing well once more.

Use this book to work out where you may be at risk of burnout and how, instead, you can create sustainability, living a life full of energy and motivation. Use the activities in this book to create a vision for how you will harness your aspirations for your work and personal life in combination with a healthy balanced perspective on it all.

Part

1

Burnout

Activity: Where are you on the road to burnout?

Could you be burning out? How do you feel right now?

Mark yourself on the scale below from 1 to 10 where 1 is 'I'm great, no problems at all' and 10 is 'I feel horrendous. I'm burnt out'.

I feel great								I'm burnt out	
1	2	3	4	5	6	7	8	9	10

Activity: What's increasing your risk of burnout?

Now let's see if the evidence matches your answer to the question above. Burnout is the result of failing to manage the stressors in your life and over-driving yourself. It's perfectly possible to be approaching burnout without realising it.

Which pressures in your life are stressing you? These could be events and people in your work or home life but could also be from within yourself as your own personality, beliefs, thoughts and emotions can create unrealistic pressure.

1. On a scale of 1 to 10, where 1 is none and 10 is high, how much tension and strain do you currently feel?

None								High amount	
1	2	3	4	5	6	7	8	9	10

2. Tick the activities that could be adding unwelcome pressure on your life.

The work you do	Tick
High workload/multiple demands on your time Unachievable targets Unrealistic deadlines and time pressures Highly pressurised environment Working out of your comfort zone – lacking skills Micromanaged, lacking empowerment Multiple managers with conflicting expectations Role ambiguity/unclear expectations Feeling undervalued	

The work you do	Tick
Lack of support by manager/colleagues	
Poor supporting resources	
Challenging clients/colleagues	
Uncontrollable, distracting activities at work	
Poor work relationships	
Boredom/unchallenging work	
Isolated from others either physically or mentally	
Work climate rife with office politics and gossip	
Being bullied	
Kept in the dark on business developments	
Excluded from decision making	
Constant uncertainty/change; continually moving goalposts	
Long/difficult commute to and from the workplace	
Work environment not conducive – open plan office, hot desking, nowhere to park	

The person you are	Tick
Career-driven	
Over-achiever	
Compulsion to prove yourself	
Highly ambitious	
'Fire in the belly' motivation	
Perfectionist	
Taking a mistake as a personal failure	
Control freak	

Part

1

Burnout

The person you are	Tick
Overly conscientious	
Overly competitive	
Taking criticism to heart	
Taking activity to the extreme, such as over-training for a marathon	
Overloading yourself	
Always striving for the next thing – project, promotion	
Can't say 'no'	
Wanting to please everyone	
Finding it difficult to switch off	
Negative thinker	
Conflicting personal/work values.	
Finding it difficult to prioritise	

Lifestyle	Tick
No time to exercise	
Disturbed sleep/lack of sleep	
Health worries	
Money worries	
Over-committed to too many people	
Lack of balance between activity and recovery	
Low mental resilience and ability to cope	
Poor social life	
Insufficient income for outgoings	
Worried by uncertainty	
Family worries	

Lifestyle	Tick
Excess use of alcohol, cigarettes, coffee, drugs Neglecting your personal life – it's all about work Neglecting health issues and avoiding the doctor	

3. How would you summarise what you have learnt from completing this exercise? What are the key stressors in your life?

Part

1

Burnout

Part 2
The body:
adrenal health

3: The mighty adrenals

Do you

- Have trouble waking up and pulling yourself together to get up in the morning
- Need something like caffeine to get you going, and caffeine hits during the day to keep you on your feet
- Often crave something salty, sweet or fatty
- Feel a bit better after lunch but then have a mid-afternoon energy crash
- Suddenly feel better about 6pm, and the feelings lasts until 9pm or 10pm… but then you're exhausted
- Get a second wind which could keep you up until 1am or 2am in the morning if you don't go to bed as soon as exhaustion hits?

If this is frequently your daily routine, then there's a good chance you may be experiencing adrenal fatigue. The good news is that you can turn this around and recover your energy and motivation for life.

Activity: How exhausted do you feel?

On a scale of 1 to 10, where 1 is 'awake and fully energised' and 10 is 'exhausted', how do you mostly feel?

Awake and fully energised									Exhausted
1	2	3	4	5	6	7	8	9	10

The mighty adrenals

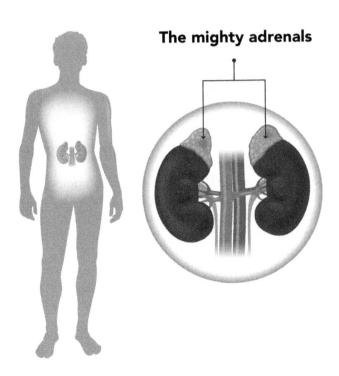

Here's the science: some background to the mighty adrenals. If science isn't your thing, give it a go. Understanding what's happening is the first step to managing it.

What are the adrenals?

The adrenals are two tiny triangular shaped glands attached to the top of each kidney. Their function is to produce and secrete a variety of hormones. These hormones give commands to the organs and tissues in the body which give us the energy and capacity to cope when faced with sudden or heightened pressure, challenges and trauma.

There are two parts to the adrenal gland – the medulla (inside the gland) and the cortex (outside of the gland). Each part produces particular hormones.

1. The medulla releases the hormones **adrenaline** and **noradrenaline**. These stimulate our 'fight or flight' response.

2. The cortex produces:

    - **cortisol**, a steroid hormone which regulates and modulates the changes in the body that occur in response to stress, regulates the level of glucose in the blood and the metabolism of protein, carbohydrates and fats.
    - **aldosterone**, which maintains the body's salt and water levels, protecting us from dehydration. This regulates blood pressure and fluid retention.
    - **oestrogen, progesterone and testosterone**. These are also produced in much larger quantities by the ovaries (in women) and the testes (in men).

But this description doesn't go anywhere near describing how vital, mighty and powerful the adrenals really are.

Our adrenals are vital to survival

The primary function of the adrenal glands is to enable you to deal with trauma, shock and danger. Your adrenals are critical for your survival.

Just imagine hearing some bad news. You might be worrying about a bill that needs paying; you could be struggling to manage the pressures of a deadline; you could even have suffered an injury playing sport. It may be

Part
2

The body: adrenal health

as basic as low blood glucose levels, so that your brain needs more fuel to function.

What happens?

When something concerns, shocks, stresses or challenges you, your adrenals are instructed by the brain to produce and release a whole cascade of hormones. These hormones will generate a variety of changes in the body to help you deal with the perceived danger. It's called the 'fight or flight' response (I'm sure you've heard of it before). You fight the danger – or you run away faster than you ever thought possible. One of those two responses is vital for your survival.

This fight or flight response is also called the 'stress response'. This stress-response is a very finely-tuned process.

Any sense of panic, danger or trauma will be picked up by two parts of the brain:

1. **The amygdala**. This is located deep within your subconscious, 'primitive' brain. It processes your memories and emotional reactions using your experiences, recollections, values, opinions and feelings to make quick decisions, particularly those related to survival.

2. **The cerebral cortex (cortex)**. This more recent evolution for humans is located just behind the forehead. It's where you do your conscious logical and rational thinking and manage learning, language and memories.

Both these areas of the brain will perceive and trigger a response to danger. However, for survival purposes, the rather impulsive amygdala will respond faster than the slow and measured thinking of the cortex, so the amygdala tends to take over subconsciously.

A whole cascade of hormone reactions takes place:

- the amygdala interprets the messages that come into the brain
- if it perceives a threat, it sends a distress signal to a gland at the base of the skull called the hypothalamus

The hypothalamus acts rather like a dispatch centre, receiving information then sending out signals simultaneously to:

- your nervous system (the neurones in your brain and the complex network of nerves running from your spinal cord that transmit signals to specific places in your body) using electrical impulses in nerve pathways to trigger the release of adrenaline from the adrenal medulla

- your endocrine system (a collection of glands around your body that produce hormones to regulate the activity of cells and organs) using the bloodstream to stimulate cortisol from the adrenal cortex

It is the combination of these two systems that generates the 'fight or flight' (stress) response.

A specific part of the nervous system is used for 'fight or flight'. This is the **autonomic nervous system** which automatically controls the function of many of your organs, muscles and glands such as the heart, lungs, stomach, intestines, bladder and sex organs.

The autonomic nervous system is divided into two subsystems:

1. The sympathetic nervous system: the 'fight or flight' ON switch
2. The parasympathetic nervous system: the 'fight or flight' OFF switch

Part

2

The body: adrenal health

Sympathetic System

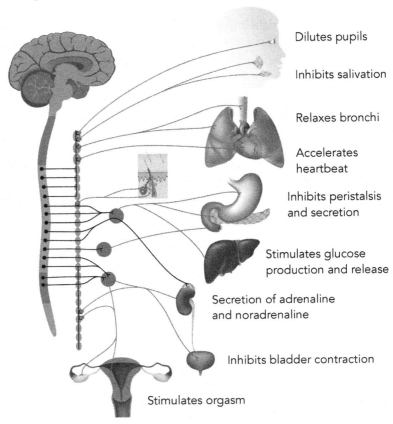

Dilutes pupils

Inhibits salivation

Relaxes bronchi

Accelerates heartbeat

Inhibits peristalsis and secretion

Stimulates glucose production and release

Secretion of adrenaline and noradrenaline

Inhibits bladder contraction

Stimulates orgasm

The sympathetic nervous system (illustrated in the diagram above) triggers the 'fight or flight' stress response.

When in danger, the body needs to react in an instant. Thanks to the nervous system and adrenaline, it does so – it's like slamming your foot on the accelerator. Instantly, the car accelerates.

Changes in your physiology prepare you physically and mentally to deal with the danger you face.

It's your 'on switch', making changes in your body that keep you alert, give you a burst of energy and prepare you for action when you're in danger.

'Fight or flight' activities include:

- dilating your pupils
- focusing your attention
- raising your blood pressure
- tensing your muscles
- slowing your digestive system
- suppressing your immune system
- instructing your liver to release stored glucose so that your muscles have the energy to respond

When the danger is over, there's also the body's 'off switch' which returns it to its resting self. This is called the parasympathetic nervous system.

Parasympathetic System

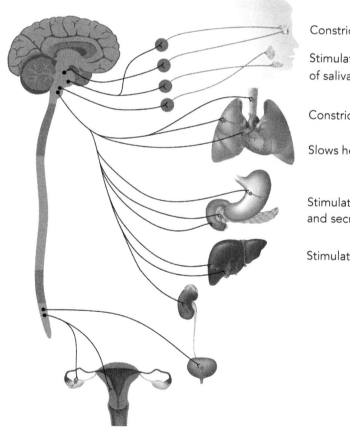

Constricts pupils

Stimulates flow of saliva

Constricts bronchi

Slows heartbeat

Stimulates peristalsis and secretion

Stimulates bile release

Part

2

The body: adrenal health

The parasympathetic nervous system (illustrated in the diagram on the previous page) is about rest, recovery and digestion. The heartbeat slows, blood pressure lowers and digestion fires up again.

This enables the body to return to a state of relaxation which allows you to recharge ready to face the next demand, whenever it comes.

The HPA axis response

When the hypothalamus stimulates the endocrine system, it first signals the pituitary gland (which lies just behind the bridge of the nose), to release hormones to trigger the adrenals. The adrenals then secrete stress hormones to set off the changes in the body which are necessary to manage the danger you're experiencing.

This cascade of hormones might seem complicated, but it is a very efficient process. It can be summarised as the **HPA axis: hypothalamus – pituitary – adrenal axis.**

Combined with the activation of the sympathetic nervous system, the HPA axis is life-saving. When in danger, the body needs to change in an instant and thanks to the nervous system and adrenaline, it does.

Staying balanced

'Fight or flight' is like a light bulb which is either on or off. When activated, the light bulb comes on, heats up and lights your way to safety. When the danger passes, the light bulb switches off, cools down and allows you to relax, recover and recharge.

Alternating between 'on' and 'off' is important. One should not dominate. If it does, it will be at the expense of the other.

Firing up the sympathetic nervous system prepares you to cope with a threat. But if you get stuck here, typically because you're living with unmanageable pressure, there is no opportunity to rest and recover.

Putting our bodies under chronic stress

The challenge for Young Professionals is that this very clever system evolved to protect us when we lived in a time of on/off danger. If a wild animal was standing on the path in front of you, you had to decide very quickly whether to run away or fight it. Once dealt with, the danger was over so your body could relax and calm down.

It's not like that today. Firstly, we are facing ever-increasing pressures and demands. Our primitive brains flag these up as life-threatening dangers.

Secondly, the more we have to deal with, the more we have swirling about in our heads. We relive problems from the past and worry about the future. This over-activates the mind and creates intolerable tension.

Cortisol is the hormone which regulates the way the body changes in response to stress. If your body consistently experiences stress and therefore often requires cortisol, your adrenal glands will prioritise cortisol production. Facing real pressures and challenges as well as being worried, anxious and having a lot on your mind locks you into a state of **chronic stress.** This means your amygdala is instructing the hypothalamus to **over stimulate** your nervous and endocrine systems to enhance the 'fight or flight' response.

Stuck in permanent 'survival mode'

Our bodies are very adept at survival. Although information comes into the cortex (the thinking brain), this performs at a much slower rate than the instinctive amygdala. Conscious rational thinking and analysis take time.

The amygdala works rapidly, using emotions and memories to make a quick decision about the best course of action to save your life. To do this, cortisol temporarily 'shorts out' the cortex so all responses come from the amygdala.

To save your life, the amygdala works on a principle of **act first, think later!** It has the advantage of receiving information twice as quickly as the cortex to be fair, the cortex stands little chance.

Your body signals danger. Straight away, the amygdala instructs the hippocampus to mobilise the adrenal army. And because it uses memory and emotion to identify risk, the amygdala cannot distinguish what is

Part 2

The body: adrenal health

life threatening and what is not. This means that everything is treated as dangerous. Now you're in permanent 'survival mode'.

If your body continues to require cortisol for quite some time, then to conserve energy and stored nutrients (such as vitamin C) the adrenal glands will prioritise its production to adrenaline and cortisol. You become stuck in what I call 'always on'. You're producing ever-increasing amounts of cortisol for a danger that isn't really there. You're also blocking the activation of the parasympathetic nervous system which would relax you and return you to a balanced state.

In other words, you've left your light bulb on and it never switches off. The longer you continue like this, the sooner the bulb will wear out. That's burnout.

What does cortisol do to you?

Cortisol is secreted in a 24-hour rhythmic pattern. It peaks in the morning as you first wake, to give you a surge of energy and motivate you for the day. This then tapers off until it is low enough to allow you to sleep at night.

However, this natural rhythm becomes disrupted by chronic stress, which stimulates a relentless cascade of stress chemicals to keep you on high alert. This makes it hard for you to spend time in a calm and relaxed state and to provide your body with the time it needs to recover.

Twenty first century living, which keeps you under constant pressure and gives you little down-time, creates a big problem for your body. Stress can be very bad for your health.

Humans evolved to manage short, intermittent bouts of danger. We did not evolve with the capacity to be relentlessly stimulated, with little opportunity to switch off. The trouble is that we are unable to distinguish between real danger – for example when someone is about to attack you – and being in a constant state of stress because of deadlines or having too many things to do.

Producing this cascade of hormones helps you to cope with stress, but eventually, the adrenals become weary and unable to make enough hormones to meet the demand. The result is you find it increasingly difficult to respond to stress and cope. Like any machine, if used for too long doing what it was not designed to do, the system eventually breaks down.

Because the autonomic nervous system governs the heart, lungs, stomach, intestines, bladder and sex organs, being stuck in 'fight or flight' puts these organs in an unnatural state that is really only sustainable for a short time. Being in this state for an extended time, without rest and recovery, puts you at risk of various health conditions. These get worse the longer you are stuck. In many cases, it can leave you with life-long complaints.

The effects of chronic stress

Although the effects of stress are not inevitable, stress does increase your risk of the following:

- poor immune function, leading to allergies, autoimmune conditions (asthma, Crohn's Disease, Hashimoto's thyroid disease) and cancer

- raised blood pressure and cholesterol and blood vessels constricted by the 'fight or flight' response, leading to cardiovascular disease

- over-stimulation of the hormone insulin, needed to manage blood sugar levels, leading to insulin resistance and eventually Type 2 diabetes

- 'yo-yo' levels of cortisol, leading to low energy, dry hair and skin and lack of concentration

- slowed digestive system (you have no time to eat or digest when you're in danger), leading to symptoms of Irritable Bowel Syndrome (IBS - stomach cramp, bloating, diarrhoea and/or constipation), and the possibility of a stomach ulcer

- suppressed immune system in the gut, compromising the gut's flora balance and leading to allergies, food intolerances, candida overgrowth and bowel diseases such as Crohn's or coeliac disease

- brain fog, poor memory and concentration affecting performance and output

- migraines and headaches

Part

2

The body: adrenal health

– anxiety disorders, depression and dementia caused by the toxicity of high levels of cortisol in the brain

– insomnia caused by high cortisol inhibiting sleep

– prioritising cortisol secretion over sex hormone production, leading to a low sex drive, PMT, infertility (men and women), pre-menstrual tension and menopausal symptoms (women)

– weight problems, particularly abdominal fat, caused by sugar imbalances and sugar and fat cravings

Activity: What effect is stress having on your long-term health?

Adrenal dysfunction is a progressive condition. You deteriorate from full health... end up with ill-health... then eventually go into burnout.

1. Look at the diagram below. Are you experiencing any of these symptoms and conditions?

Brain: depression, anxiety, insomnia, low energy, migraines

Neck: hypothyroidism, sore throats, mouth ulcers

Hair: hair loss, thinning

Muscles & Joints: pain, tension, fibromyalgia, fluid retention

Arteries: high blood pressure, cholesterol, stroke

Lungs: coughs, colds, asthma

Heart: heart disease, irregular heart beat

Liver & Pancreas: liver disease, diabetes

Stomach: ulcers, malnutrition, anorexia, constipation, IBS, IBD

Sex glands: PMT, irregular periods, low libido, prostatitis, night sweats

Weight gain: fat around the middle

Skin: ageing, acne, rosacea, eczema, psoriasis, allergies

2. List any symptoms and conditions you are experiencing here.

Activity: Your reflections

Now is the time to reflect on your thoughts and the activities you have completed in The Mighty Adrenals chapter.

Has anything particularly struck you as interesting? Review the chapter in light of the following questions and record your answers below:

- What have you learnt about yourself in this chapter?
- What do you need to change?
- What do you need to start doing that you have not done before?
- What other thoughts do you have?

4: The road to adrenal fatigue

Your adrenals have a normal daily rhythm of manufacturing and releasing cortisol.

When we first wake up in the morning, we release a surge of cortisol into the bloodstream. Cortisol is a stimulatory hormone, which gives you the 'oomph' to get up and get going. You continue to naturally release cortisol for the rest of the day, but in ever diminishing amounts. Eventually, come the time when you want to go to sleep, levels will be low enough to allow this to happen. This is a normal cortisol rhythm.

When you have a stressful day, instead of releasing diminishing amounts of cortisol, your adrenals react by ensuring that the amount of cortisol released remains elevated. This helps you cope – you're in 'fight or flight' stress mode.

However, if this continues day after day, without giving yourself time to switch off and recover, your adrenals and the receptors around the body that receive the cortisol hormone will have been overworked and become exhausted and unable to function sufficiently. When this happens, you can no longer produce enough cortisol to meet your demands to cope, so cortisol levels remain low all day.

Fired - Wired - Tired

It is helpful to consider this in terms of three stages:

- Stage 1: Fired – a state of good mental and physical health with a normal cortisol rhythm.
- Stage 2: Wired – a state where we feel enduring 'strain' and where cortisol levels are elevated.
- Stage 3: Tired – a state of 'crash' and burnout with low levels of cortisol.

Let's look at these stages in more detail.

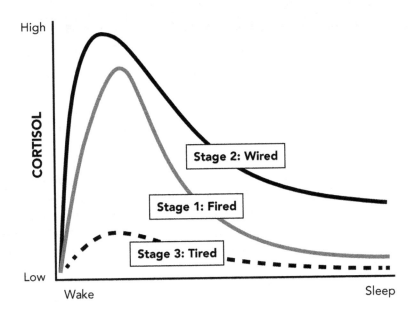

Stage 1: Fired

Case study

Myra was loving her job as a lawyer. Yes, it had its challenges, not least the workload, but she was feeling good.

The last few weeks had been a bit tough, though. Myra was working on a client project with a very tight deadline. There were penalty clauses written into the contract, so all stops were being pulled out to deliver it successfully. In fact, the project leader had asked if everyone working on the project would come into work on the next four Saturdays as well, so they could really focus on it without the distractions and interruptions of normal office life.

Myra felt that if her career was going to progress, she couldn't refuse, but she was concerned about what it might do to her physically. She was also worried about her relationship with her boyfriend, which was still in its early stages. She was enthusiastic about the opportunity to be working on this project and knew there was no point in being miserable and annoyed about how it would impinge on her outside work time; she needed to take the good things from it that it was giving her.

As this was a new and exciting project, Myra decided to keep a log of how it progressed. She asked lots of questions and recorded these in her log. She made sure she told all her friends that she'd be off the scene for a few weeks and asked them to bear with her. She swapped her Pilates class to a Sunday lunchtime. She even stopped off at a shop on the way in on Saturday and bought some fruit for everyone to share.

Yes, it was hard keeping a six-day week going, but she coped well. Thanks to the various rituals Myra put in place, she felt she was still in control of her life.

This is a good example of Stage 1, where Myra was in a state of good mental and physical health.

The most important aspect is that she felt in control and was able to cope and maintain her performance. It would be quite normal for there to still be moments of tension, but by having rituals in place, she quickly dealt with these and regained control.

*Myra was in a state of **'normal cortisol rhythm'**. Her cortisol peaked when she first woke up and had tailed off by the time she was ready to go to bed.*

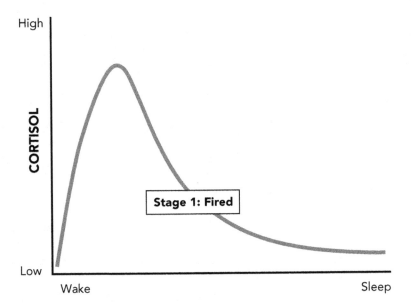

Normal cortisol rhythm
- Blood sugar is balanced
- Food is digested well and absorbed into the bloodstream
- The immune system is fighting infections well, so few episodes of flu or nasty viruses occur
- Cuts and abrasions heal well
- Blood pressure is normal (unless there is another medical condition present)
- Cholesterol is normal (unless there is another medical condition present)
- The mind is clear and focused
- Sleep is sound and long
- Muscles are toned and relaxed
- You feel full of vitality and energy

Stage 2: Wired

Case study

Jack was fed up. His Irritable Bowel Syndrome (IBS) was back again and was getting worse. To be honest, all he wanted to do was to curl up on the sofa but he knew this wasn't possible.

A colleague had been off sick for some time following surgery and Jack was picking up as much of his colleague's job as he could. He wasn't used to some of the processes, so everything took longer than it should have done. This left him feeling panicky about how he would keep on top of his own job.

Jack had his annual appraisal looming and he knew a customer had made a complaint about him. It was ridiculous, he just hadn't had the time to return the customer's phone calls. If he was honest with himself, that wasn't the only mistake he'd made... but he thought he had got away with the others.

Jack had recently taken the decision to opt out of football training, although he loved the exercise and the social aspect of getting together for a drink afterwards. Now he was finding that the only way to chill at the end of a day was to have a few beers at home. It also meant that this freed-up time could be put to good use getting on top of his workload.

Jack wasn't sleeping that well either. He found himself waking in the middle of the night and couldn't get back to sleep again. He wondered why it was that when you've been so tired, your mind still wakes you with your to-do list at 3.30am? It didn't make sense, but he supposed it would sort itself out eventually, just like everything else – he just had to get used to it all.

The body: adrenal health

This is a common example of Stage 2, where Jack had been experiencing too much pressure. He could function and even have some reasonable days, but it was taking more and more effort.

Mentally and physically, he wasn't feeling too good, and was struggling to cope and maintain his standards. It was becoming harder to concentrate at times and he wasn't performing as well as he knew he could. He went to work, but the reality is that he was there in body but not mind.

This is what we call 'presenteeism' and it not only affects your performance, it also impacts the efficiency, output and relationships of your team, particularly if others have to pick up what you're failing to do.

*This is also a state of **'heightened cortisol rhythm'**. The adrenals have been over-stimulated for quite some time, resulting in high levels of cortisol throughout the day. The physical changes modulated by cortisol leave you feeling 'Wired', as if your mind and body are always on the go.*

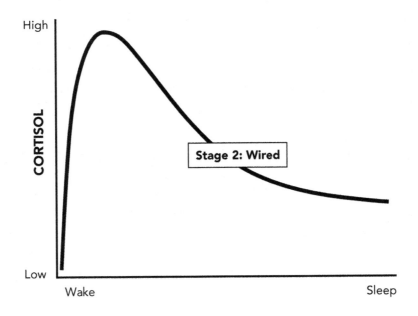

Heightened cortisol rhythm
- Blood sugar is imbalanced so energy fluctuates. You experience cravings for stimulants such as coffee and alcohol and fat storage increases around the middle
- Digestion slows so digestive symptoms appear – IBS (stomach cramp, bloating, diarrhoea and/or constipation), heartburn, indigestion

- Immunity is suppressed so colds, bugs and infections take hold
- Blood pressure is high due to elevated aldosterone levels which may spark headaches, palpitations or visual problems
- Cholesterol and blood fats are elevated, leaving you feeling foggy
- Cognitive function is impaired. You feel hyped-up, yet it's hard to concentrate and remember things. You may suffer anxiety or panic attacks
- Sleep is disrupted – it's either hard to get to sleep or you wake abruptly during the night
- Muscles are tense so back pain, pulled muscles or joint pain is likely
- Loss of libido

This is a dangerous stage. When cortisol is first raised, you feel you're really performing well, and it gives you a 'buzz'. But the buzz that cortisol gives is addictive – so the path to burnout generally goes unnoticed.

The cortisol effect is like an iceberg – 90% invisible!

90% of the effects of high cortisol go undetected as they're happening 'under the surface' – rather like an iceberg lurking beneath the water. With the body stuck in this 'Wired' state, lots of the changes that are meant to be protective now begin to generate health problems.

These can include insomnia, IBS, back pain and even depression. It's really important to recognise the warning signs at this time, and avoid going into denial about what's starting to happen. Once you slide into burnout, recovery is much harder.

Yet typically, it's during Stage 2 that symptoms are ignored. It's because this is the hardest time to free yourself from the demands you're experiencing. Also, excess cortisol blocks activity in the cerebral cortex where you do your reasoning and judgement.

Taking time out to relax and recover is of the utmost importance when you're Wired. I cannot emphasise it enough. This is the time to stop and take stock.

Part
2

The body: adrenal health

Listen to those around you who may be telling you 'you don't seem yourself right now'. You may well benefit from seeing your doctor or pharmacist for a health check (a personal MOT).

Coping when you're Wired

If you're in a state of heightened cortisol rhythm where cortisol remains elevated, then it's critical that you make yourself as physically resilient as you can. Stress places an added burden on your body, burning up vital nutrients and putting you at risk of malnourishment, so what and how you eat can have quite an impact on you.

When you're Wired, you crave quick energy fixes (sugar and fat) which makes it easy for your diet to go haywire. It's therefore important to make an extra effort to eat healthy, nourishing food.

Diet and lifestyle tips

- Eat small, regular meals, with a healthy morning and afternoon snack to balance your blood sugar.

- Eat whole grain carbohydrates, with good quality white meat or vegetable protein (chicken, turkey, quinoa, lentils and beans).

- Eat a variety and abundance of vegetables to top up nutrients and antioxidants.

- Avoid salt and increase your intake of potassium-rich foods such as avocado, bananas, beans and lentils, mushrooms, fish and dark green leafy vegetables such as spinach and kale. This is because aldosterone levels are high which increases sodium and lowers potassium in the cells, raising blood pressure.

- Eat fresh fish, but avoid other fat as cortisol is made from cholesterol; you want to reduce this.

- Avoid caffeine and alcohol completely as they stimulate cortisol, increasing the burden and affecting your sleep cycle.

- Make sure you eat regularly. If you're going to be stuck in a meeting over lunch time, it's better to have an early lunch at 11-11.30am than go too long without eating.

- Undertake enjoyable exercise that includes social contact. Exercise raises the heart rate, clearing the toxic load that's building up from high levels of brain activity, increases energy and reduces excess stress hormones, leading to increased feelings of happiness.

- Laughter is the best medicine. Make a point to smile regularly throughout the day and when appropriate, laugh! Laughter decreases stress hormones, and your body relaxes.

- Sleep! It's so important for repairing your body and processing emotions from your day. Have some rituals to aid this: take a bath in the evening, turn off digital technology at least 90 minutes before bed or practice some calming breathing exercises.

Part
2

The body: adrenal health

Stage 3: Tired

Case study

Chris's company had moved location about a year ago. It was an awkward location to get to from where he lived, so he drove into London each day. He got up at 5.30am, made himself a bowl of muesli, covered it with berries and seeds, ate it and hit the road.

That was the last substantial and healthy thing Chris had to eat each weekday. His workload left him little time to get out to buy a sandwich at lunchtime, so he grabbed a few biscuits when he felt peckish and kept the coffee cup topped up.

His day was long but he was mostly coping with the demands. He was aware he was rather irritable with people... but that was just because he was busy and distracted.

On his way home, Chris would stop off at the gym for an hour. He couldn't understand why he was putting on so much weight when he hardly ate anything. This meant he didn't get home until after 9pm. His flat mate had eaten, so Chris had another bowl of cereal, then went to bed... and so, the whole routine started over again the next day.

Then one day Chris was in a meeting and a director was pressuring him for an answer. Suddenly, he just couldn't think straight. He was sweating and confused. He hardly knew his name. He felt emotional, vulnerable and very, very frightened.

The work doctor was called to see him. His company medical insurance paid for him to spend time in a private hospital to address his fragile mental health. He was there for four weeks and left the hospital rattling from a cocktail of anti-anxiety and antidepressant pills and all the side-effects that went with these meds. He was off work for six months and even though he later returned, his tolerance for any pressure had diminished.

This is a real-life example of Stage 3.

Chris simply could not continue at this pace indefinitely.

When over-stimulation of the adrenal glands continues without taking time out to regain an equilibrium, there comes a time when they can no longer operate to the desired level – and so he crashed.

This isn't necessarily caused by work stress. You might have increased the burden on your body by training for a marathon, or perhaps have a chronic health condition, both of which add to the stress response.

The adrenals still work – but not well enough to produce the levels of cortisol necessary to manage the strain you're experiencing. You feel so exhausted that even sleep can't help. You're unable to cope and function, and have zero tolerance for dealing with even minor problems. This is called **'diminished cortisol rhythm'***... in other words, you're now in burnout.*

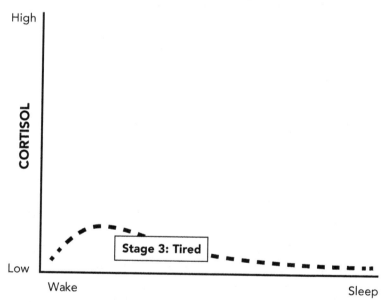

Part

2

The body: adrenal health

Diminished cortisol rhythm
- Low blood sugar levels lead to low energy and sugar cravings
- Low blood pressure so you may feel dizzy upon standing
- Craving salty food
- Often craving fatty foods as cholesterol is required to make hormones
- Allergies and food intolerances
- Sleep is erratic
- Poor cognitive function makes it hard to think straight

- Feeling low and depressed
- Poor immune function making you susceptible to every bug going around the office
- Headaches or migraines
- Swollen ankles which are worse in the evening
- Muscles and tendons are weak and ache as they have become inflamed. Joint pain, frozen shoulder or tennis elbow is a possibility
- Poor sex drive, infertility issues, menstrual irregularities, PMT or menopausal symptoms

Coping when you're Tired

Diet is fundamental when treating burnout. Begin with the changes you find the simplest to do, waiting until you get stronger before you making changes you may find more challenging.

- **Watch what and how you eat.** Eat a varied, healthy diet and set aside time to eat regularly. Do not miss meals.

- **Balance your blood sugar.** When adrenally fatigued, it is essential that you balance your blood sugar. Low blood sugar levels stimulate the stress response, adding a further burden to your adrenals.

- **Eat regularly:** three meals and two healthy snacks each day
  - Avoid refined carbohydrates such as white bread, white pasta or white rice. Replace them with brown rice, whole wheat pasta or bread
  - Eat something by 10.00am. Your body has been fasting overnight and needs fuel or it will activate the stress response to raise blood glucose levels
  - Always eat whole grains and combine these with some good quality proteins at every meal. This might include chicken, turkey, fish, eggs, dairy, quinoa or beans and lentils. Protein slows the digestion of carbohydrates and so helps slow their absorption
  - Avoid caffeine which stimulates the release of cortisol (the stress hormone)
  - Have a small snack before you go to bed to maintain blood sugar levels through the night. It might be a small piece of chicken or tinned salmon or hummus on an oatcake
  - Try to avoid sugary drinks such as squash, fruit juice, fruit smoothies, cola and energy drinks, even if you're craving them

- **Eat 'good' oils.** Top up your healthy oil consumption by eating fish and nuts and seeds: use olive, hemp or rapeseed oil to make dressings.

- **Hit your five-a-day target for veg servings** – and beat it if you can. Eat at least five to six portions of vegetables every day. Variety is key, so include lots of colour (dark green, red, orange, yellow, purple). Vegetables are a rich source of vitamins, minerals and antioxidants, providing the nutrients the body requires to manage the extra demands that it's experiencing.

- **Keep fruit to a minimum.** It's high in natural sugar which upsets blood sugar balance and in potassium which will upset your body's salt/water (electrolyte) balance.

- **Use salt.** To rebalance your electrolytes, salt your food to taste. But avoid table salt. Instead, use Himalayan rock salt or sea salt which both contain minerals. Also, minimise potassium-rich foods such as bananas, beans and dried fruit as low aldosterone affects levels, lowering blood pressure.

- **Eat foods high in B vitamins.** The manufacture of adrenal hormones requires B vitamins, so eat good sources of these such as vegetables, whole wheat bread and pasta, and grains such as brown rice.

- **Avoid:** sugar, caffeine, fruit juices, hydrogenated fat, junk and processed food.

- **Take some gentle exercise** but avoid competitive sports. Gentle swimming, walking, dancing or cycling are all good. Exercise at a pace that does not leave you feeling more tired the next day and most importantly, is enjoyable. Start slowly and build it up, but don't let it stress you!

- **Try a Tai Chi or Hatha Yoga class.**

- **Take a walk in the daylight.** This stimulates the feel-good hormone serotonin, which is converted to melatonin, the sleep hormone, in the evening.

- **Go to bed early (before 10.30pm)** – whatever you do, don't sit up late with a second wind.

Part
2

The body: adrenal health

Testing for adrenal fatigue

Burnout is caused by excessive stimulation of the adrenal glands due to excessive pressure. Here are a couple of tests you can do to identify how your adrenals may be functioning.

Test 1: Blood pressure check

Lie down for ten minutes and relax. Have a blood pressure monitor prepared and towards the end of the ten minutes, take your blood pressure. Stand up and take another reading immediately. A drop-in blood pressure may be an indicator of adrenal fatigue.

Test 2: Pupillary check

Rest in a darkened room for about one minute, then shine a pen light across the pupil of your eye and look in a mirror to see whether the pupil contracts, as it should do. If it contracts and remains contracted for 30 seconds, then your adrenal health is good.

If the pupil cannot hold the contraction and begins to pulsate, contracting then dilating then contracting, then this is a sign that the muscle is low on glucose reserves, and your adrenals are not so good. If the pupil pulses initially then dilates, despite the light still shining on it, then this is a sign of adrenal fatigue.

Test 3: Salivary cortisol tests

Go to www.youngprofs.net to order an Adrenal Stress Profile test kit. This test measures cortisol levels in your saliva collected four times over the course of one day. A detailed report will illustrate your results and how to improve them.

Activity: Where are you on the road to burnout?

If you were to take a 'helicopter view' of your life, what would you see?

The road to burnout brings psychological and physiological symptoms (mind and body) which vary from person to person. What are you experiencing?

1. Read the signs and symptoms of each stage and tick the ones you notice in yourself.
2. Add up the number of ticks and record them in the relevant box at the bottom.

Behaviours

Stage 1: Fired **Fired is characterised by healthy engagement**	Tick
Excited and motivated by work. Nothing is too much trouble	
Feel in control despite the demands you're experiencing	
Feel professional and personal life are well balanced and able to switch off from work when at home	
Able to meet the demands of your job well and performing well	
Mind is sharp and able to focus and concentrate on the job in hand	
Able to make decisions as and when required	
Able to identify and work on the key priorities at work whilst also being flexible should situations change	
Managing and balancing your time well	

Part

2

The body: adrenal health

	Tick
Finding time to enjoy being with friends and family members	
Can control your moods and emotions well	
Others feed off your energy and passion. You may even energise the mood in the room when you're there!	
Have a positive perspective on life, feeling anything is possible	
Eating healthy foods and allowing time to for eating	
Do not have the need to use coffee, cola, alcohol, cigarettes, caffeine pills to function	
Feel physically fit and healthy. Taking time to exercise and monitor own health	
Total ticks:	

Stage 2: Wired Wired is characterised by over-engagement	Tick
Having to work hard to maintain energy. Feel weary at times	
Beginning to lose control and your capacity to cope with internal and external demands. You don't like to admit it, though	
Over-identifying with work; finding it difficult to let go	
Performing less well, even making mistakes, so have to work harder to achieve personal high standards	

	Tick
Memory, concentration and focus seem compromised at times	
Procrastinate more, so experience difficulty making decisions	
Find it hard to identify real priorities; everything seems urgent and important, so may let people down	
Getting up earlier to get more done, often because of difficulties maintaining sleep	
Isolating oneself from friends and family to get on top of work Can be cold and distant with colleagues	
Becoming insensitive to others, irritable, short and snappy, possibly even sarcastic. Losing your sense of humour	
Deny there is a problem when your nearest and dearest question your behaviour	
Seeing the cup as half empty as negative emotions take over	
Changes in eating habits. Craving quick energy foods and grabbing food on the go	
Self-medicating heavily to keep going – coffee, cola, alcohol, cigarettes, caffeine pills, sleeping pills	
Struggling with health issues: IBS, migraines, insomnia, high blood pressure, back pain, chronic fatigue, depression	
Total ticks:	

Part

2

The body: adrenal health

Stage 3: Tired Tired is characterised by disengagement	Tick
Overwhelming mental and physical exhaustion. Feel utterly drained and wrung out which isn't relieved by sleep. Difficulty rising in the morning	
A complete loss of control: you feel exhausted, demotivated, helpless	
Loss of all identification with work. Saddened at the thought of what this might be doing to your career	
Unable to cope with any demands. Do the minimum to just get through	
No mental function – cannot think straight, focus or remember much	
Everything seems overwhelming and insurmountable	
Organisational skills gone to pot – missing deadlines, ignoring priorities and just about able to cope with simple tasks	
Cannot pull yourself together to function	
Feel indifferent to life, people and work. It feels very lonely but you can't cope with much else, so shut yourself away	
Feel emotionless but negative and irritable with others	
Self-neglect or change in appearance with a change in washing and dressing habits	

	Tick
Feel worthless – what value do I have now this has happened? Sceptical and critical	
Eating is erratic. Possible cravings for salt and/or sugar	
Not much appetite for anything	
Many health issues including low blood pressure. Possible anxiety and depression	
Total ticks:	

So, where do you have the most ticks?

If you have more in 'Fired' then you are more likely to be fired up and full of productive energy. That's good! But if you have more in 'Wired', this gives cause for alarm as you're beginning to struggle with the demands and pressures. And if most are in 'Tired', then you're now experiencing burnout and urgent action is required.

3. Consider what has changed in your life that may have led you to being Wired or Tired. Think back:

    a. When did you start to feel this way?
    b. What was going on in your life at the time and what has been going on subsequently?
    c. Do you want to continue on this path?
    d. Do you want to do something about it?
    e. Are you willing to make the necessary changes?

It's **your** choice whether you burn out, not that of your employer or your manager! Although they may have created the conditions, it is **your** mindset and reactions that make the difference. You must create a more realistic perspective on life and on your personal capabilities and limitations.

Take control and make the necessary choices that engage you in the activities that will help you manage the conditions. You have a choice to act or not act – but if the warning signs are there, can you afford to ignore them any longer? Once you crash, it's impossible to know just how far-reaching the result will be, except that it will be utterly miserable for you and those who are close to you.

Activity: Your energisers and drainers

Now that you understand what burnout is, how it affects you and where you're at, let's move on to some ways of reflecting on your life and managing your situation. Remember, I did say that you can have your cake and eat it!

Read these carefully and choose the activities that are doable for you without causing you extra stress.

1. What and who currently are the things in your life that are good for you? Record everything you can think of in the Energisers column. Consider diet, lifestyle, people, events, relationships, personal attitudes and beliefs.

   Note: this is about what you have right now, not what you think you should have.

Energisers	Drainers

2. What and who are the things in your life that are bad for you, that drain you, stress you and spark off negative feelings and emotions? Record these in the Drainers column.

3. If there is something you think could be recorded in both columns, put it in both but try to distinguish the difference that makes it either an Energiser or a Drainer overall.

4. Mark the top 5 items in each column and rank them from one to five.

5. Look at the Drainers column and reflect on the following questions:

    a. Why are these Drainers so significant?
    b. What specific aspect of each Drainer is draining you?
    c. What impact are these Drainers having on your life?
    d. What can you do to diminish the impact of Drainers or remove them completely from your life?

    The reality is that you have three choices to improve your life.
    i.   To take action and change the situation.
    ii. To change yourself to adapt, for example by reframing how you perceive things.
    iii. To accept the situation and ignore it.

6. What can you do to have more of the Energisers in your life?

Activity: 360 feedback

One of the symptoms of being 'Wired' is that you lose your self-awareness. But this is a time when you really cannot afford to be blinded. Make an effort to find out how others view you, your attitudes and your behaviour right now. Are they noticing any recent changes?

1. Seek the opinions of family, colleagues, associates.
2. What are they telling you, that you may not have been aware of?
3. What is this telling you? Review the exercises again in this section to identify your risk of burnout.

Part
2

The body: adrenal health

Activity: Stress log

If you are experiencing stress, it may be helpful to identify the source of your stress and how you're responding.

Use this chart for one week to keep a record.

Date	Time	Activating event or situation	How did you feel?	What did you do?	What were the consequences?

Activity: Creating a balanced life

'The time to relax is when you don't have time for it'.
Sydney J. Harris

In other words, if you don't have time to switch off, then you should take it as a sign that your sympathetic nervous system is becoming stuck in the 'on' position.

Relaxing and taking time to recover should not be confined to the end of the day when you're at home from work; you need to be taking opportunities to do this throughout the day.

Balance is not a 'nice to have' but a 'must-have' if you are to avoid burnout.

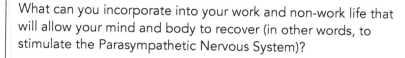

What can you incorporate into your work and non-work life that will allow your mind and body to recover (in other words, to stimulate the Parasympathetic Nervous System)?

1. At work

2. Out of work

Part
2

The body: adrenal health

67

Activity: Your reflections

Now is the time to reflect on your thoughts and the activities you have completed in The Road to Adrenal Fatigue chapter.

Has anything particularly struck you as interesting? Review the chapter in light of the following questions and record your answers below:

- What have you learnt about yourself in this chapter?
- What do you need to change?
- What do you need to start doing that you have not done before?
- What other thoughts do you have?

5: Other factors affecting adrenal health

Other factors affecting adrenal health

It's not only stress that affects adrenal health, although this is the main culprit. Other lifestyle factors also trigger the release of cortisol. Examples include:

- A poor diet high in refined carbohydrate and fat, and low in nutrients
- Blood sugar imbalance
- Stimulants such as caffeine, alcohol, cigarettes and drugs
- Lack of or broken sleep
- Allergies and food intolerances

- Poor gut health – such as yeast, bacteria, parasitic infections, low levels of beneficial bacteria
- Toxic overload such as parabens, silicates, mercury, lead, nickel
- Low grade infections

To optimise your adrenal health, you need to consider your life as a whole. This includes your diet and lifestyle – it's not just about work at the office.

You are what you eat

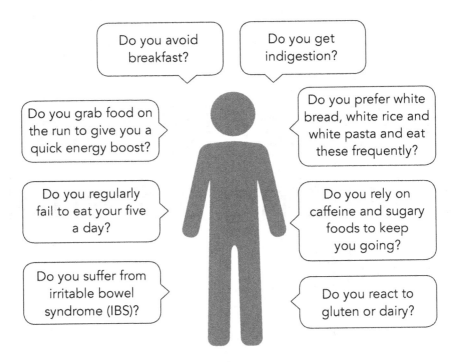

If you have answered Yes to any of these questions, then you need to read this section.

Stress depletes nutrients and the sad fact is that with modern farming methods, many fresh foods are lower in nutrients than they have been in the past. This means that a modern diet can fail to deliver the basic recommended daily allowance of nutrients.

If you want healthy adrenals, you need a rich varied diet supplemented with vitamin and mineral nutrients. Here are a few basic rules:

1. **Nutrient levels are vital:** During times of high stress, your body has a high demand for certain nutrients. If you don't eat the right foods, these nutrients can become depleted and your adrenals will struggle to function.

   - It's a simple recipe: eat foods high in vitamins B and C. These nutrients are predominantly found in fruit, vegetables and whole grains.
   - Avoid processed foods – what I call beige foods – such as white bread, white pasta and white rice which have had the nutrients stripped out during processing.
   - Don't eat the same foods all the time. Think variety and think rainbow – the more colourful your food, the more nutrients you are taking in.

2. **Take time to eat.** If you want to absorb nutrients from your food, you need to take time to do so:

   - Whatever you do, don't bolt your food down on the run. Calm, mindful eating allows your digestive system to do its job without being influenced by stress hormones which slow it down.
   - Focus on your food. Be mindful of what you are eating, not the problem you have at work that you need to rush back to.

3. **Get yourself some good gut bacteria:** High levels of cortisol reduce the good bacteria in your gut. This is because the sympathetic nervous system slows digestion. These good bacteria, such as lactobacillus and bifidobacterium, play an important role in the absorption of nutrients, protect you from food sensitivities and promote healthy immune function.

To build up yours:

   - Eat prebiotic foods which contain inulin or fructo-oligosaccharide (FOS) as these are a food source for good bacteria and help improve the numbers of good gut bacteria naturally.
   - Eat probiotic foods that contain good bacteria such as natural live yoghurt, kefir, and sauerkraut.

Part

2

The body: adrenal health

4. **Be aware of food sensitivities and allergies:** Food sensitivities, such as gluten (found in wheat) and casein (found in dairy) stress the body, activating the stress response.

  - If you suspect a food intolerance, (the most common are wheat, dairy, yeast and soya), cut **one** suspect food out of your diet for two weeks and see how you feel when you reintroduce it. Never cut more than one food type out at a time – you won't know what is causing the problem and I'm not in favour of eliminating too many food groups, as you need a varied diet. This will require you to vigilantly check food labels as these ingredients are often hidden in unexpected foods.

5. **Eat organic:** Where you can, I encourage you to eat organic foods, as fruit and vegetables are heavily sprayed with chemicals during the growing period. If you cannot, always wash all fruit and vegetables well before eating them.

6. **Stay hydrated.** The brain requires water to function properly, so becoming dehydrated negatively affects your ability to cope.

  - If you wait until you're thirsty to drink, you're already dehydrated. Instead, drink small amounts of fluid regularly and check that your urine remains a pale yellow colour.

To prevent burnout, you need an adrenal-friendly kitchen stocked with a variety of food types as listed below:

Nutrient	Food source
Vitamin B: Needed to produce cortisol and maintain energy levels, particularly B5 B vitamins include: B1 (thiamine) B2 (riboflavin) B3 (niacin) B5 (pantothenic acid) B6, folates, biotin	Whole grains – whole wheat, wheat germ, rye, barley, oats, brown rice, wild rice Green leafy vegetables – greens, kale, spinach, Brussels sprouts, broccoli Mushrooms Eggs – free range Nuts – almonds, Brazil nuts, sesame, walnuts (unsalted and not heat treated) Seeds - sunflower, pumpkin, sesame, hemp, Chia, flax (unsalted and not heat treated)
Vitamin C: Supports adrenal gland function, the production of cortisol adrenal recovery. Stress increases the excretion of vitamin C	Citrus fruit – oranges, grapefruit and lemons, but not neat fruit juices Berries – blackberries, blueberries, raspberries, strawberries Other fruit - kiwi fruit Salad - red and green peppers, watercress, tomatoes Vegetables - broccoli, peas, sweet potato, pumpkin, vegetable juices such as V8

Part
2

The body: adrenal health

Nutrient	Food source
Minerals: calcium and magnesium: Help to relax and calm the mind and body	Magnesium – green leafy vegetables (broccoli, cabbage, kale, spinach), almonds, Brazil nuts, pumpkin seeds, sesame seeds and pineapple Calcium – dairy products, spinach, seeds, sardines
Good fats (Omega 3, 6 and 9): Help support immunity and reduce inflammation caused by stress	Oily fish – salmon, trout, mackerel, fresh tuna (not tinned) Nuts – almonds, Brazil nuts, sesame, walnuts (all unsalted and not heat treated) Seeds – sunflower, pumpkin, sesame, hemp, chia, flax (all unsalted and not heat treated) Eggs from chickens fed on a diet rich in omega 3 oil: these are stocked in a number of supermarkets Avocados Oils – extra virgin olive, hemp, walnut, coconut Nut butter – cashew, almond
Lactobacillus and bifidobacterium: Good bacteria for the gut	Prebiotic foods – Jerusalem artichokes, chicory root, leeks, onions, asparagus Probiotics foods – Live, unsweetened natural yoghurt, kefir (fermented milk drink), sauerkraut (fermented cabbage), tempeh and miso (fermented soybean), kimchi (spicy fermented cabbage)
Theanine Helps you relax by increasing alpha waves in the brain	All tea without milk, but particularly green tea

Nutrient	Food source
Water: To keep the body and mind hydrated and functioning	Water: about 8 glasses of water a day, or 1.5 litres. Herbal and fruit teas – chamomile, liquorice and passionflower

Supplements

Here are some basic supplements for adrenal support. You are not expected to take them all. A good multi vitamin and mineral is a good start. Consider seeking the advice of a nutritional therapist.

For information about stockists, visit www.youngprofs.net

Nutrient	What it does	What to take
Multi vitamin and mineral	A good variety of vitamins and minerals helps to prevent any deficiencies caused by the extra demands on the body	A multi vitamin and mineral
Vitamin B complex and extra B5	Supports adrenal function, particularly vitamin B5 (pantothenic acid)	High strength B vitamin complex plus 500 mg B5 (pantothenic acid)
Vitamin C	Stress increases the excretion of vitamin C yet it is needed for the manufacture of cortisol	Take 500mg twice a day

Nutrient	What it does	What to take
Calcium/ magnesium	Nature's tranquilliser. Helps calm you and is a benefit if feeling anxious	600mg calcium and 400mg of magnesium during the day, or if finding sleep difficult or feeling anxious, take one hour before bed. Take together in a supplement which also contains Vitamin D to aid absorption by the body
Digestive enzyme	Aids digestion and nutrient absorption as stress slows the digestion process. Good if experiencing bloating after a meal, or indigestion	One tablespoon of apple cider vinegar before a meal or one betaine hydrochloride or one digestive enzyme with each meal. Avoid betaine hydrochloride if you have a stomach ulcer

And for extra support:

Nutrient	What it does	What to take
Phosphatidyl serine	A chemical which helps to bring down high cortisol levels, quietening the mind and reducing the 'Wired' feeling	Take 30 minutes before bed
Probiotic	Live bacterial and yeasts available in capsule form that may help improve the microflora in the gut and provide health benefits	Take according to manufacturer's instructions. Keep in the fridge once open. If you are taking a digestive enzyme, as described above, don't take this at the same time
Adrenal glandulars	Protein from adrenal gland extracts which provides nutrients to rebuild and repair the glands without hormones. Helps to revitalise overworked glands	Begin very gently with half to one tablet a day with meals then build up according to manufacturer's instructions
Theanine	Helps you relax by increasing alpha waves in the brain	100mg three times a day

Part

2

The body: adrenal health

Nutrient	What it does	What to take
Taurine	Relaxing amino acid similar in structure and effect to the calming brain chemical called GABA	500-1000mg twice a day plus same amount of glutamine to support GABA production
5-HTP	Helpful if mood is low. **Avoid if on any antidepressant medication**	100mg twice a day in two doses 50mg and build up to 300mg over a day
Adaptogenic herbs	Perform as a general tonic for the adrenals by strengthening and balancing them whether they are over or under performing	See suggestions below

Adaptogenic herbs:

Nutrient	What it does	What to take
Ginseng	Performs as a general tonic for the adrenals by strengthening and balancing them whether they are over or under performing	If male: Korean Ginseng (panax) 100mg 1-2 times a day for 2 months. If female: Siberian Ginseng 200mg 1-2 times a day for 2 months. Take care not to overuse, as this can cause insomnia, irritability and anxiety as well as raising your blood pressure.

Nutrient	What it does	What to take
Licorice (glycyrrhiza glabra) Not deglycyrrhised as no hormone action	Elevates cortisol by preventing its breakdown Rich in nutrients (vitamins B and chromium) Care needed: avoid if you have high blood pressure as this can increase it	Tincture: 5ml 3 times day Tablets: 500mg twice a day Tea: ½ teaspoon dried powder in 300ml hot water for ten minutes then strain
Reishi mushrooms (ganoderma lucidum)	Performs as a general tonic for the adrenals by strengthening and balancing them whether they are over or under performing	Reishi mushroom capsules taken according to manufacturer's instructions
Rhodiola rosea	Enhances ability to adapt to stress by altering the release of cortisol. It also improves concentration, memory, mood and immunity	200mg – 300mg standardised extract 1-3 times a day with meals for one month. Stop for one month then start again if you need to
Valerian (valeriana officinalis)	A calming herb. Enhances the activity of GABA receptors in brain. GABA is a calming chemical in the brain that counteracts adrenaline and other stimulating hormones which make you feel wired	50-100mg twice a day and up to 200mg 45 minutes before bed

Part

2

The body: adrenal health

Activity: Blood sugar balance

Tick all that apply to you from the list below.

Symptom	Tick
Do you need tea, coffee and/or cola to keep you going throughout the day?	
Do you experience sugar/carb cravings?	
Do you prefer white bread, white rice and white pasta and eat these frequently?	
Do you feel tired after eating something sugary (including refined carbs)?	
Do you find it hard to concentrate at times during the day?	
Do you sometimes feel shaky and light-headed during the day?	
Do you experience mood swings?	
Do you skip meals because you are too busy?	
Do you avoid breakfast?	
Do you grab food on the run to give you a quick energy boost?	
Do you add sugar to your drinks and breakfast cereal?	
Do you suffer from thrush infections?	
Do you get frequent niggling headaches when you haven't eaten for a while?	
Do you wake in the night hungry?	
Do you carry extra fat around your middle?	

If you answered Yes to any of these, then you are experiencing blood sugar imbalance.

One of cortisol's most important functions when you're in danger is to ensure that you have enough glucose circulating in your bloodstream to provide an immediate burst of energy for muscles should you need it to run like mad. To make this happen, cortisol instructs your liver to release the sugar it stores as glycogen into your bloodstream.

Cortisol also has another blood glucose role. The brain requires glucose for energy, so if levels fall low (this could happen during the day because it has been some time since you've eaten, or at night-time when you're asleep), the adrenals will release cortisol to boost supplies in the bloodstream from where it is stored in the liver and fat.

As too much glucose can be toxic for the cells and brain, your body has a finely tuned feedback mechanism that warns when glucose level rises too high. When this happens, your pancreas gland swings into action and produces extra insulin to store excess glucose as fat.

The blood sugar rollercoaster

If your meals are irregular and you're under uncontrollable pressure, your adrenals will be working hard to ensure that blood glucose levels are increased. If this happens but the glucose is not used, then insulin will do its job... to store it all away again.

As this cycle of flooding the blood supply with glucose then taking it away again continues, you start to experience highs and lows in your energy levels. It's happening because the adrenals will stimulate enough glucose for you to run or fight, but in reality, you don't need this much. The extra insulin produced by the pancreas then marches in and quickly reduces the amount of glucose in the blood stream, leaving you feeling low.

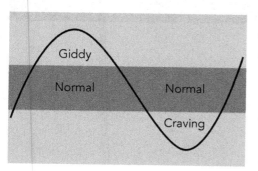

When levels are low, you crave foods that will give you a quick surge of energy again – typically refined carbohydrates which are quickly broken down and absorbed into the bloodstream. This shoots blood glucose levels higher than required and so insulin appears again to correct things... and then your energy drops so you crave anything that will give you a quick boost again.

It's like you hitting the accelerator hard but your body then hits the brakes just as hard, so you respond by hitting the accelerator hard again and your body hits the brakes hard again, and so it goes on.... and you become more and more tired, which stresses your body more and more... so on top of this, your adrenals are being over stimulated.

These highs and lows in blood sugar mean that nothing quite knows whether it is coming or going - including you. You've taken a ride on the **'blood sugar rollercoaster'** which, despite its name, is no fun at all. Look at the chart below for the signs of high and low blood sugar.

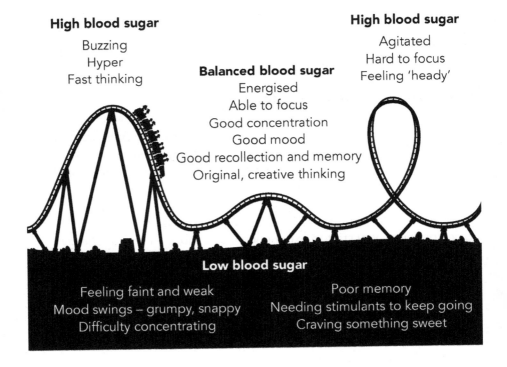

High blood sugar
Buzzing
Hyper
Fast thinking

Balanced blood sugar
Energised
Able to focus
Good concentration
Good mood
Good recollection and memory
Original, creative thinking

High blood sugar
Agitated
Hard to focus
Feeling 'heady'

Low blood sugar
Feeling faint and weak
Mood swings – grumpy, snappy
Difficulty concentrating
Poor memory
Needing stimulants to keep going
Craving something sweet

When blood glucose is high...

- you feel giddy and heady
- it may be difficult to focus
- the frequent stimulation of insulin puts you at risk of Type 2 diabetes
- your clothes don't fit as you're storing more fat (particularly around the middle)
- you experience mood swings

When blood glucose is low...

- you crave stimulants and quick fix high energy foods
- you feel tired and grumpy
- your body produces stress hormones which create further imbalances in your blood sugar

Not all carbohydrates are the same

The advice to just 'avoid carbs' is too simplistic. Complex carbohydrates such as whole grain rice or whole wheat bread (natural, unprocessed carbohydrates) still contain fibre. Fibre slows their digestion. It means they are absorbed into the bloodstream at a slow and steady rate, sustaining your energy for longer. Carbohydrates such as beans and lentils also contain protein which slows digestion and absorption.

Fruit contains a slow release form of glucose called fructose. Fructose is easily absorbed but has to make a visit to the liver on the way to your cells to convert it to glucose.

Simple carbohydrates, on the other hand, are like rocket fuel. They will send your blood sugar shooting up.

To get off this ghastly roller-coaster ride, you need to create a more sustainable balance in blood sugar levels. This starts with diet:

1. Eat the right type of carbohydrates which can be broken down in the digestive system and absorbed into the bloodstream in a slow and steady manner, rather than a frantic rush.

Part

2

The body: adrenal health

2. Include in your meals other food groups such as protein and fat, which slow the breakdown of carbohydrate food further. These foods include lean meat, oily fish, eggs, cheese, yoghurt, chickpeas, lentils, whey protein powder, nuts and seeds.

Activity: Sustainable fuel vs rocket fuel

If you feel you 'need' stimulants, experience energy slumps, find it difficult to concentrate, feel dizzy or crave something sweet during the day, it's a sign that your blood sugar levels have dropped. You need to eat, but to avoid climbing onto the blood sugar rollercoaster, you need to eat well.

Different foods affect blood sugar levels to different degrees. How is your diet affecting your blood sugar levels?

1. Think about what you ate yesterday.

2. Go systematically through the chart below and record in the Tally Box how many times you ate these foods.

3. Then add up each column and see whether your overall diet was boosting or draining your energy.

Sustainable fuel	Tally	Rocket fuel	Tally
Wholemeal sliced bread, pitta, rolls Pumpernickel Rye bread Oatcakes Porridge Whole wheat pasta Brown rice Brown basmati rice Whole grains (quinoa, buckwheat, bulgur wheat – when cooked al dente) Green leafy vegetables (kale, spinach, broccoli, courgette, green beans) White vegetables (cauliflower, cabbage, radishes) Mushrooms Salad (lettuce, cucumber, rocket, watercress, peppers, tomatoes) Fruit (berries, cherries, plums, apples, pears, oranges, grapefruit) Pulses (lentil, chickpeas, beans) Lean meat		White sliced bread, rolls, baguette Croissant, bagels, crumpets Cheese crackers White rice cakes Breakfast cereals Cake, pastries, doughnuts, scones, waffles Sweets, biscuits, cookies, chocolate bars Crisps, popcorn White, corn and rice pasta White rice Pizza Vegetables (potatoes, parsnips, swede) Chips, mashed potato Low-fat processed foods (mayonnaise) Fruit (over-ripe bananas, grapes, pineapple) Dried fruits (apricots, cranberries, dates, figs, sultanas) Fruit-flavoured yoghurt Fruit in sugar syrup Jam, jelly	

Part 2

The body: adrenal health

Sustainable fuel	Tally	Rocket fuel	Tally
Fish		Puddings, such as	
Eggs		mousse, fruit pies	
Cheese		Table sugar	
Nuts (almonds,		Ice cream	
Brazils, walnuts)		Fruit squash, fruit juices,	
Seeds (pumpkin,		smoothies	
sunflower, sesame, chia,		Tea, coffee	
linseed/flax, hemp)		Hot chocolate	
Plain yoghurt		Fizzy drinks (cola,	
Tea (Red Bush, herbal		lemonade etc)	
and fruit teas)		Energy drinks such as	
Water		Lucozade, Red Bull	
		Alcohol	
TOTAL		TOTAL	

Activity: The blood sugar rollercoaster

The blood-sugar rollercoaster can seriously impact your energy, mood and productivity. If you experience extreme highs and lows in energy during the day which eventually turn into an energy slump, then complete this exercise.

Take some time to consider how you feel at different times of the day and what you have eaten.

1. Record on the chart below:

	Early Morning	Late Morning	Lunchtime	Early Afternoon	Late Afternoon	Evening
How did I feel?						
What did I eat during this period?						

Part 2

The body: adrenal health

2. Is how you are feeling because you are hyper and buzzing, or because you are low and craving? Give the strength of this feeling a score. For example, if you feel you're buzzing or agitated, is this feeling very strong (in which case score a 5) or weak (then score a 1)? If you feel faint and weak, or maybe you're craving something sweet, how strong is this feeling? Score -5 if it is a very strong symptom and -1 if it is a weak symptom. Put an X in the square on the chart below that represents your scores to create a rough illustration of your personal blood sugar rollercoaster.

SCORE	Early Morning	Late Morning	Lunchtime	Early Afternoon	Late Afternoon	Evening
5						
4						
3						
2						
1						
Balanced						
-1						
-2						
-3						
-4						
-5						

1. Before you identify some changes you can make, ask yourself the following and record your answers in the right-hand column:

How many times a week do you skip breakfast?	
What is your typical breakfast?	
How many glasses of water do you drink each day?	
What are you most likely to drink as a pick-me-up?	
What are you most likely to snack on?	
How often do you eat carb-rich foods at lunchtime?	
What type of bread, rice and pasta do you eat?	
How many days a week do you eat 5 servings of fruit and veg?	
How many times a week do you eat oily fish such as salmon, herring and mackerel?	

Part
2

The body: adrenal health

2. Review the Stop and Replace chart below. Place a tick in the column by the foods you feel able to change.

Stop or reduce...	√	Replace with...
Branded cereals such as corn flakes or puffed rice		Porridge, home-made sugar free muesli, shredded wheat or natural live yoghurt and some berries
White toast and jam/honey/ marmalade		Boiled egg and whole meal toast
White bread sandwich, roll or baguette		Sandwich using whole meal bread/pitta/wrap or rye bread
Baked or mashed potato		Brown or basmati rice, mashed sweet potato
Sugary snacks – crisps, biscuits, popcorn, chocolate bar, pretzels		Small handful of nuts or seeds, some vegetable sticks with hummus or guacamole or a piece of fruit
Rice cakes or cheese crackers		Oatcakes
Fruit yoghurt		Plain yoghurt and add frozen berries
Cola, lemonade, energy drink		Fizzy water with lemon or lime juice squeezed in
Coffee, strong tea or hot chocolate		Coffee alternative, fruit or herb tea or water

3. What changes are you going to make to your diet to balance your blood sugar and prevent the blood sugar rollercoaster?

Stop eating/drinking	Start eating/drinking

Top tip: To remain motivated, make small and gradual changes to your diet. Choose one change per week or make the next change once you are comfortable with your previous change.

If you are reducing caffeinated drinks, reduce consumption gradually over a period of two weeks.

Part
2

The body: adrenal health

Activity: My three-day food diary

It can be more helpful to review what you have eaten over a three-day period.

1. To do this you will need to make a record of everything you eat and drink. Use the chart below. Be honest, because this will help you identify why you may feel low in energy. It may be that you are not eating enough.

Day 1	What I ate	Time
Breakfast		
Lunch		
Dinner		
Snacks		

Day 2	What I ate	Time
Breakfast		
Lunch		
Dinner		
Snacks		

Day 3	What I ate	Time
Breakfast		
Lunch		
Dinner		
Snacks		

2. Look at the chart below to get some ideas on what you can eat each day that will provide you with energy and nutrients and balance your blood sugar.

Breakfast ideas

Porridge with berries or grated apples and ground seeds

Sugar-free muesli with nuts and seeds and cinnamon

Unsweetened yoghurt and berries

Boiled or poached egg with whole wheat toast or mushrooms

Poached egg with spinach

Scrambled egg and smoked salmon

French toast made with whole wheat bread

Hard-boiled egg and Parma ham

Nutribullet smoothie with added flax seeds and chai seeds for protein

Protein shake

Part 2

The body: adrenal health

Lunch ideas

Greek salad

Salad nicoise

Tomato, mozzarella and avocado salad

Mackerel, horseradish and beetroot salad

Omelette/frittata with Parma ham and mushrooms or red peppers

Wrap with chicken, fish or hummus and salad

Food from previous evening's meal

Brown rice or quinoa or can of lentils with mixed chopped peppers, tomato, cucumber, beetroot and feta cheese

Homemade soup with meat and lentils

Tinned salmon and cucumber open sandwich made with one slice of bread

Dinner ideas

Chicken or pork casserole with onions, carrots, celery

Roast meat and roast or mashed sweet potatoes and green leafy vegetables

Chicken and noodle stir fry

Cottage pie with sweet potato topping

Lamb chop with roast sweet potatoes and salsa verde

Homemade meat or vegetarian curry with wild rice

Salmon en papillote with chopped celery and tarragon and asparagus, new potatoes

Baked cod on lentils and peppers

Lentil and chickpea curry

Stuffed red peppers

Snack ideas

Few unsalted nuts

Small palm-full of seeds

Oatcake with hummus or nut butter

Ryvita and cottage cheese

Oatcake with cheese

½ whole wheat pitta bread and mackerel pate

Small piece of cheese and an apple

Small plain yoghurt and fruit

Carrot and celery sticks with hummus or guacamole

Celery and nut butter

Hard-boiled egg

Cold meat – chicken

Roll of smoked salmon

Protein shake made with coconut milk

Further tips to avoid the Blood Sugar Rollercoaster

- **Monitor how you eat when you're feeling stressed.** This is the time you're more likely to crave simple carbohydrates and stimulants to give you a lift (and save time on eating!).

- **Always eat breakfast.** Your body has been fasting for ten to twelve hours and needs glucose, otherwise it stimulates the stress response. If you can't face anything first thing, have something when you get to work and always eat before 10.00am.

- **Plan your meals in advance** and use left-overs from the previous evening's meal for lunch, rather than buying a sandwich.

- **Make time to eat and don't get hungry!** You need to eat regularly to balance your blood sugar. Eat three meals a day, and have a small snack in the morning and afternoon.

- **Avoid adding sugar to your food or drink** – sugar provides empty calories. If you add sugar to your tea or coffee, gradually reduce it each week until you have none.

- **Reduce the amount of fruit juice and fruit smoothies** you drink (apple, orange, pineapple, even freshly squeezed orange juice). Smoothies give a faster sugar rush than natural fruit because they have had the fibre removed, so the sugar is quickly absorbed by the body. Initially, dilute smoothies until you can eventually give them up.

- **Avoid foods with added sugar:** 'healthy' snack bars, free-from foods, low-fat foods, tinned soups, baked beans, sauces and fruit yoghurt are often laden with sugar to provide flavour.

- **Avoid cola which contains caffeine and sugar:** a double whammy. Energy drinks often contain caffeine to give a boost but seriously affect blood sugar balance.

- **Check labels.** When you buy ready-made food products, check the label for sugar content. Avoid foods with anything over 5g of sugar per 100gm of food. Five grams is equivalent to one teaspoon.

- **Avoid artificial sweeteners** found in low calorie drinks. Artificial sweeteners trick the body into thinking we've had something sweet when we haven't. We therefore crave sugar and look elsewhere to get it. As a result, we can end up eating far more of it. Such products confuse the body and stress it.

- **Avoid or keep to the minimum any alcohol.** It's high in sugar!

- **If you're still craving sugar,** see a nutritionist. It could be a sign of a yeast/candida infection in the gut or low levels of serotonin, a chemical in the brain.

Helpful foods

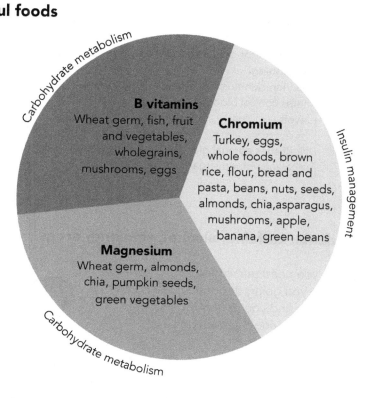

Carbohydrate metabolism

B vitamins
Wheat germ, fish, fruit and vegetables, wholegrains, mushrooms, eggs

Chromium
Turkey, eggs, whole foods, brown rice, flour, bread and pasta, beans, nuts, seeds, almonds, chia, asparagus, mushrooms, apple, banana, green beans

Insulin management

Magnesium
Wheat germ, almonds, chia, pumpkin seeds, green vegetables

Carbohydrate metabolism

You can also consider the following supplements:

Nutrient	What it does	What to take
Chromium	Helpful for insulin and blood sugar management. Helps you get off the blood sugar rollercoaster and manage cravings. It is a vital ingredient of glucose tolerance factor which helps insulin carry glucose from blood into cells	400-600mcg per day of chromium picolinate or polynicotinate (better absorbed) Take in morning to balance blood sugar
Magnesium	Plays a role in carbohydrate metabolism so helps to regulate blood sugar levels	500mg once a day with food.

Part
2

The body: adrenal health

Nutrient	What it does	What to take
B vitamins	Important for carbohydrate metabolism. B3 (non-skin-flushing niacin) helps control blood sugar levels	Take a B complex plus 30mg niacinamide B3 (make sure it is non-flush)
Adaptogenic herbs	Nourishes adrenal glands to rebalance blood sugar	See previous explanation on page 78-79 for suggestions

The stimulants: caffeine, alcohol, smoking, drugs

- Do you need tea, coffee and/or cola to keep you going throughout the day?
- Do you find you're drinking more alcohol during the evenings and at weekends?
- Do you need something to help you switch off from the day?
- Are you finding it difficult to give up smoking?
- Are you becoming reliant on over-the-counter drugs or illegal drugs?

If your answer to any of these is Yes, you could be addicted to stimulants.

We know that stress leaves us feeling out of control and cortisol upsets our blood sugar balance. When either of these things happen, we are more likely to turn to a stimulant to help us cope and feel we're back in control again.

Using stimulants leads to burnout

Let's take coffee. Coffee provides no calories so it can't provide energy. Instead, it stimulates our liver to release stored glucose for energy production. This process requires the release of stress hormones (adrenalin and cortisol) so we put ourselves into a state of stress to get some energy to function and deal with the stress we are already experiencing! This isn't good for you.

Coffee also gives you a lift for about an hour by triggering dopamine, a chemical in the brain which feeds your need for a reward. Once the effects of the coffee have worn off, you feel low and crave another one and so the cycle continues.

It's the same with all the other stimulants. They all stimulate the stress response. That's what's giving you a lift in energy and focus.

But all this is doing is taking you further along the road to exhausting your adrenals and burning out.

Activity: Are you addicted to stimulants?

1. Look at the stimulants listed in the left-hand column, and record the number of times you used each stimulant listed during the course of a day.

Stimulant – per unit	Tally of units per day	Alternative
Caffeine • Tea – 1 cup • Expresso – ½ shot • Americano – 1 cup • Cola – 1 cup • Red Bull – 1 can • Caffeine pills – 1 pill • Dark chocolate – 70g • Milk chocolate – 200gm		**Tea:** • Reduce the strength or use a smaller mug • Try Red Bush tea or herb or fruit tea **Coffee:** • Reduce by one cup per day per week • Try Barleycup, Yannoh, Caro, dandelion coffee as an alternative **Energy drink** (cola, Red Bull, Lucozade): • Gradually reduce until you have cut out **Chocolate** (bars or drink): • Replace with carob snacks or drinks

Sugar • In hot drink – 1 teaspoon • Cake – per half portion • Biscuit – per portion • Sweets – per sweet • Hidden in foods – per 5gm		Gradually cut back the amount you add to hot drinks, one teaspoon each week • Replace sugary cereals with suggestions in the menu chart • Avoid dried fruits – have a piece of fruit instead • Dilute fruit juice, then give it up • Check labels for added sugar • Avoid sugar substitutes
Alcohol • Beer, lager, cider – per ½ pint • Wine – per 80ml glass • Spirits – per 25ml measure • Mixers – per mixer		• Ideally have an alcohol-free month while you're rebuilding your energy Otherwise: • Have alcohol-free days during the week • Cut out drinking at lunchtime • Set yourself a weekly goal of the maximum number of units • Drink a glass of water between each alcoholic drink to reduce overall consumption
Cigarettes • Per cigarette, cigar		Get support to reduce from your doctor or local hospital
TOTAL UNITS PER DAY		

2.   Add up the total number of units. If your energy levels
     are good, then you are allowed 2-3 units before it would have
     a detrimental effect. If you experience low energy and you
     want to improve your energy, your score needs to be zero until
     you feel your energy improve. Look at the right-hand column
     above and determine what you can do to lower your
     stimulant score.

What can I do to lower my score?	When will I do this?

Top tips to minimise your intake of stimulants

- **Reduce stimulants gradually.** They're like a drug – you'll be addicted and withdrawal will leave you with a headache if you come off them too quickly.
- **Decaffeinated coffee still contains two stimulant chemicals** so swap it for fruit and herb teas or coffee alternatives. Red Bush tea is popular because you can add milk to it.
- **Green tea** is high in caffeine but it also contains theanine which is a relaxant which outweighs the caffeine.
- **Avoid alcohol.** Although you might feel relaxed, alcohol is actually a stimulant which also contains high amounts of sugar, disrupting your blood sugar and making you crave high carbohydrate foods.

A good night's sleep is essential

Sleep, said Thomas Dekker, is the golden chain that ties health and our bodies together.

- Does it take you longer than 20 minutes to switch off and fall asleep?
- Do you wake abruptly in the night – and then your whole to-do list floods your mind?
- Do you regularly experience disturbed sleep?
- Do you need an alarm to wake you most mornings?
- Do you still feel unrefreshed and groggy when you get up?

If you've answered Yes to any of these, then continue reading.

A good night's sleep is essential if you're going to stand any hope of preventing burnout. Yet it's highly likely that if you are experiencing sleep disturbances, it's because you're overloaded and struggling to cope with all the demands life is throwing at you.

Lack of sleep has a big impact on the adrenals, disrupting your cortisol rhythm. As we've learned, cortisol affects mood, memory, concentration and focus. A disrupted night's sleep allows the emotion-centred amygdala to take over, overpowering the logical cortex, and making you more sensitive to the unwelcome challenges and pressures you're experiencing. This increases the demands on your already overworked adrenals.

To put further pressure on the adrenals, sleep disturbance also causes blood sugar imbalances. Just losing out on one good night's sleep affects your hunger hormone, ghrelin. It's all about survival. Feeling drowsy, forgetful and unfocused makes you vulnerable and leaves you hungry and craving for quick energy food. You eat far more than usual because leptin, which tells your brain you are full, is suppressed when you haven't slept well.

Getting out of sleep debt

Eating too late, particularly if it's a heavy meal, drinking a caffeinated drink or alcohol or doing high intensity exercise two hours before bedtime, stimulates cortisol which disrupts the dream part of our sleep cycle, called rapid eye movement (REM).

You might feel that such late night activities relax you and help you fall asleep, but the chances are they don't. Because they stimulate cortisol, your blood sugar balance is impaired, your blood sugars fall too low in the night then a surge in cortisol to restore blood sugar wakes you.

Long-term sleep disruption has serious health consequences by weakening your immune system, putting you at risk of autoimmune conditions.

I hear so often: 'If only I didn't have to sleep! It's such a waste of time'. But let me tell you, it's not – it's a vital process that returns you to a balanced state. Sleep is all about rest, restoration and repair and it's critical if you want to be able to think clearly, concentrate, deliver effectively, interact well and appreciate the life you have. Yet so many live their lives in a state of sleep debt.

Your body has evolved to be very busy while you sleep, restoring you back to balance:

- You release growth hormones to help you grow muscle and repair the damage caused to the body during the day
- Your liver detoxes toxins
- Your mind processes the emotions you've built up during the day by dreaming, using metaphor and imagery to process it
- You consolidate and embed your memories from the day from short-term to long-term memory
- The cerebral spinal fluid that surrounds your brain and spinal cord clears the by-products from the brain cells' activity that day

Part

2

The body: adrenal health

Research tells us that the optimal amount of sleep for health is 7-8 hours per night. Stress can make this difficult to achieve; you might have trouble getting off to sleep, then you wake in the night and struggle to drop off once more. You need a regular, consistent pattern to your sleep.

And it doesn't help you at all to be sleep deprived from Monday to Friday, then sleep most of Saturday and Sunday. It can take us more than a week to recover from the consequences.

The high levels of cortisol which come with being stuck in 'always on' mode, block the production of the sleep hormone melatonin, creating a vicious cycle that raises cortisol levels further so you find it even harder to go to sleep or stay asleep. You need more melatonin to counteract the effect of cortisol. The best way to do this is to get outside in the daylight in the morning for at least half an hour. This increases the production of serotonin (the happy hormone) which is also involved in sleep because it is converted to melatonin by the brain in the evening.

Another option is to drink a glass of sour cherry juice before you go to bed. Cherries contain melatonin.

It's why mindfulness and meditation have become so useful at helping insomnia. Mindfulness reduces elevated cortisol, helping you to fall asleep faster and stay asleep for longer.

Screens can keep us awake

Something else that blocks the production of melatonin is the bluish light emitted from digital screens. If you want to sleep well, then you should shut down all computers, phones and tablets two hours before bedtime, as melatonin secretion can be inhibited for about 90 minutes. For the same reason, do not have a TV in your bedroom.

Amnesty International lists sleep deprivation as a form of torture! It isn't any wonder that with sleep being the number one casualty of living with stress, we're struggling so badly and feel on the verge of crashing out.

You know you've had a good night's sleep when you wake feeling refreshed in the morning and haven't needed the alarm clock. If this isn't the case, then it's time to take stock and identify the root cause. Is it stress, anxiety, worry, too much noise? Or maybe it's the light in the bedroom or even the blue light from the laptops and smart phones you've been using, right up until you go to bed?

Activity: What is the quality of your sleep?

If you're not getting 7-8 hours sleep, keep a three-night sleep diary to identify your sleep pattern.

	Night 1	Night 2	Night 3
How many hours did I sleep for in total?			
What did I do during the evening – eat, drink, exercise?			
How would I rate my levels of stress and anxiety during the day?			
What time did I get into bed?			
How long did it take to fall asleep?			
Did I sleep through the night?			

Part
2

The body: adrenal health

105

	Night 1	Night 2	Night 3
What times do I think I woke during the night?			
How long was I awake for?			
What was on my mind?			
How did I wake up in the morning – naturally or by the alarm clock?			
How did I feel on waking?			
Did I use anything to 'get me going'? What?			
Did I catch up on sleep during the day? When?			

We spend inordinate amounts of time using digital technology, in and out of work. Often we use it right up until the time we retire for bed, catching up on emails or keeping up with Facebook or Twitter.

If you let it, technology has the capacity to increase the length of your working day, strain your eyesight and disturb your sleep. The concentration involved certainly uses up vital energy.

Use this exercise to gain some perspective on your use of digital technology.

1. How long have you spent looking at screens over the last three days?

Consider your computer, laptop, tablet and phone or smartphone as well as your TV.

	Morning	Afternoon	Evening
Computer/laptop			
Tablet/iPad			
Phone/smartphone			
TV			

Part 2

The body: adrenal health

107

2. What actions could you take to reduce the time you spend on technology? Here are some ideas:

- Take regular breaks from your screen – 5-10 minutes each hour
- Turn off email notification and set aside a time to answer emails
- Unsubscribe from junk email
- Limit time on social media, and if conversations create negative thoughts, delete the application
- Have a digital 'sundown' when you turn off technology a certain time before retiring for bed (preferably two hours if you do not want to disturb your sleep)
- Leave your phone and tablet in the kitchen at night. The electromagnetic waves emitted can disrupt the sleep hormone melatonin

As you'll see in the top tips below, sleep isn't something that just happens. You have to plan for it by creating the right environment and following certain rituals.

Top tips for naturally inducing sleep

- **Have a weekday routine** of going to bed at the same time each night (early enough so you get some sleep before midnight when Human Growth Hormone is released) and getting up at the same time each day. Doing this will help to fix your sleep body clock.

- **Create a calming bedtime ritual** to reduce stress, prepare for sleep and set a sleep-wake rhythm. This could include switching off technology by 9pm, having a hot bath, doing some breathing exercises, reading or listening to some relaxing music. However, avoid napping in the chair before you go to bed because this will disturb your sleep!

- **Ensure that your bedroom is dark and free from noise**, and that your bed is comfortable. Wear eye shades or put up a blackout blind if there is light disturbing you, or wear earplugs if there is uncontrollable noise.

- **Cool down.** You are more likely to fall asleep when your body is cool so turn down the heating in your bedroom. Take a warm bath before bed with some lavender oil or Epsom Salts added to calm you. The ideal time is one to two hours before you'd like to retire. By this time your body will have cooled enough to make you sleepy.

- **Stay up if you're not tired.** Don't go to bed if you feel wide awake. You will feel worse lying in bed unable to sleep. If you go to bed and then can't drop off to sleep, get up and do something else.

- **Do a 'brain dump'** before you go to bed. This could include writing a to-do list for the next day or recording what's on your mind and what you can do about it.

- **Have an 'electronic sundown'.** Set a time when each evening you turn off the computer, tablet and smartphone devices. This means no emails after a certain time.

Part

2

The body: adrenal health

- **Have a massage** to relax your muscles and calm you.

- **Use 'pink noise'**: this is sound still audible to our ears but operating at a low frequency to calm the mind by slowing brain waves. Download tracks from YouTube.

- **Keep a gratitude diary.** Before you settle to sleep, record three things in your diary you are grateful for that day. This helps your mind to feel more positive about your day and reduces elevated stress hormones.

- **Use a sleep app that delivers binaural beat music.** This is music in which two sounds or tones are used to create the illusion of a third tone. The illusion stimulates alpha waves in the brain which are associated with deep relaxation.

Top tips if you wake in the night

- **Your blood sugar may be low.** Having a small snack before bed may help. Try something like a banana, or some chicken on an oatcake, as these contain tryptophan which is required to make serotonin.

- **Try meditation.** Forget counting sheep – it requires too much concentration. Try a body scan meditation where you focus on different parts of the body, tensing then relaxing, beginning at the feet and working up to the head.

- **Brain dump.** Keep a notepad by your bed to write down thoughts that come into your mind.

Healthy sleep foods

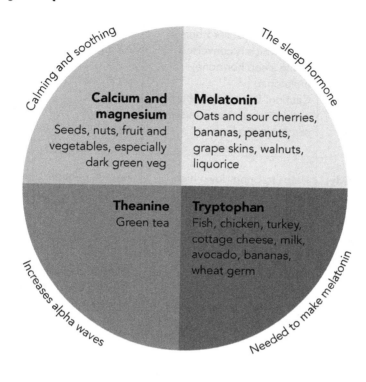

You can also consider the following supplements:

Nutrient	What it does	What to take
Calcium and magnesium	Has a calming effect and helps you relax. Often called Nature's tranquilliser	600mg calcium and 400mg of magnesium one hour before bed. Avoid carbonate versions as these are poorly absorbed
Vitamin B Complex plus B5	Support adrenal function, particularly vitamin B5 (pantothenic acid)	High strength B vitamin complex plus 500 mg B5 (pantothenic acid)
Vitamin C	In high demand when stressed	500mg twice a day

Part
2

The body: adrenal health

Nutrient	What it does	What to take
5-HTP (5-hydroxy-tryptophan)	Helps to boost serotonin levels which is converted to the sleep hormone, melatonin. Caution: Do not take if on antidepressants as it raises serotonin too high	100mg over 2 times a day or 200mg ½ hour before bed
Phosphatidyl serine	Helps to bring down high cortisol levels, quietening the mind and reducing the 'Wired' feeling	Take 30 minutes before bed
Valerian (Valeriana Officinalis)	Herb which enhances activity of GABA receptors in brain. GABA is a calming chemical in the brain which can help people get to sleep and remain asleep	50-100mg twice a day and twice as much 45 minutes before bed
Hops (Humulus Lupulus)	Calm the nervous system. Helpful if valerian is not well tolerated	200mg twice a day. 1-2ml of tincture one hour before bed. Avoid if you suffer from depression Take with valerian or Passiflora Incarnato, 100-200mg per day
Theanine	Helps to increase alpha brainwave activity which is calming	100mg twice a day, one dose 30 minutes before food and the second before going to bed

Exercise: the best booster

- Are you too tired to exercise?
- Do you find you're not able to do as much exercise as you used to do?
- Do you find it too difficult to find the time to exercise?
- Do you frequently make excuses for not exercising?
- Do you hate the gym but don't know what other kind of exercise you could take?
- Do you spend most of your day sitting at a desk?

If you've scored Yes to any of these questions, then you need to develop an exercise regime.

Exercise and stress

Exercise is a really great way to use up excess glucose, but if you are starting to struggle with managing life's demands and challenges, then cortisol levels may well be too high, and exercise will raise levels higher still. This exacerbates the impact of being 'Wired' further.

This is a Catch 22. Exercise relieves mental stress which reduces elevated cortisol but exercise causes us stress and raises cortisol!

We're regularly told that exercise is important for health – and it's true. The increase in oxygen to the brain and rise in the levels of hormones such as endorphins, serotonin and dopamine have positive effects on your mind, body, mood, emotions and happiness. This helps you to remain positive, which is an important aspect of being resilient.

Exercise also uses up excess glucose, which is why so many stressed people feel less jittery after exercise. It takes you away from the 'worry chatter' swirling around in your head, freeing you up for a time from the burden of life, which can lower cortisol levels and subsequently reduce tension and anxiety.

But exercise can also temporarily trigger the HPA axis (which was discussed in Chapter 3), pushing the body into a stress response. The more intense the exercise is, and the longer it lasts, the higher your cortisol levels will be. Endurance sports such as marathon running trigger the highest levels: that's

Part

2

The body: adrenal health

because cortisol is produced during exercise and for a short time after. In the case of marathon runners, more cortisol has been produced over a longer period of time. (Running a marathon can take 3, 4 or more hours). Cortisol gradually increases as the body adapts to the different energy requirements for endurance compared to a thirty minute jog around the park. Any exercise lasting more than 60 minutes, whatever its intensity, will significantly decrease glycogen stores, so the demand for cortisol will increase further to get you the energy you need.

How much cortisol is produced will also depend on how fit you are. If you're struggling to cope with life and usually spend your evenings slumped on the sofa but then decide to attend an aerobics class, your body will interpret what's happening to you as a danger and will release cortisol to help you cope. Your level of cortisol will be much higher than if you are fit and regularly attend that class.

The effects of exercise therefore, boil down to **duration** and **intensity**.

However, if you are to prevent burnout, there's something else you need to consider: how healthy your adrenal glands are at this point in time.

Fitness if you're 'Fired'

If you're 'Fired', it's your free choice what exercise you do. But if your circumstances change, you'll need to be mindful of any changes to your capacity to cope.

What to watch for if you're 'Wired'

If you're 'Wired', you can still exercise, as this can help you mentally and physically. But there will be limitations on type of exercise you do and for how long – for example, full marathon running would elevate what is already high cortisol further, putting you at risk of crashing. You do, however, need some sort of activity to use up the extra blood glucose circulating in your body.

It's therefore best to find exercise that keeps your heart rate below 90 beats a minute, that you find enjoyable, and that still mildly exerts you. Pace yourself, and if you feel exhausted afterwards or later that evening, this will be your body telling you that you've done too much and you need to step it back a notch.

Take it steady if you're 'Tired'

If someone has succumbed to 'Tired', then in order to recover, they must give their adrenals time to repair. Something like a competitive sport will wear them out further because it will stimulate the body to release cortisol.

Exercise therefore needs to be gentle and non-competitive as you don't have the capacity to produce the cortisol required, and this will put back your recovery. Lighter activities, such as gentle walking for a maximum of thirty minutes, do not elevate cortisol and are better for your health until your adrenals recover.

Getting started

So, if you are inactive, how do you safely get started?

You are built to be mobile, and exercise is about using your body. Physical activity does not have to mean playing competitive sport or going to the gym three times a week. It's about getting out of your chair – just moving. If you feel too tired to exercise, break sessions into ten minute slots, then fifteen minute slots and build up to one hour, three times a week. Mix and match your activity so that you don't get bored. To get and to keep the stress-reduction benefits of exercise, you need to enjoy it.

You can incorporate exercise into your everyday life by just choosing to be active - walking upstairs, cycling to work, doing lunges as you go to the photocopier. See the top tips below for ideas.

Part

2

The body: adrenal health

115

Activity: What activities have you done in the last week to raise your heart rate?

Consider all activity, such as playing football, going to the gym, swimming, dancing and tennis as well as taking the stairs instead of the lift, walking to the shops, morning stretches.

	During the day	In the evening
Monday		
Tuesday		
Wednesday		

	During the day	In the evening
Thursday		
Friday		
Saturday		
Sunday		

Activity: What could you do to become more active?

We are three times less physically active than 50 years ago. Many jobs are not as physical as they were. It's important that we don't just spend our time sitting at a desk all day, sitting as we commute and finally sitting on the sofa in the evening. To avoid the tendency of many modern lifestyles to immobility, we need to consciously plan periods of activity.

1. Read the tips list below.
2. Identify how you can incorporate exercise into your daily life. What rituals will you put in place to make sure you stick to your plans?

What I could do to exercise more?	How I will ensure I stick to it?

Top tips for incorporating exercise into your home routine:

- While waiting for the kettle or a pan of water to boil, do some press-ups using the kitchen worktop to support you. Add in a few squats or star jumps.
- While dinner is cooking, put a baked bean tin in each hand and do some arm exercises or use a sport elastic band or dumb bell if you have one. Resistance work is good for strength and tone.
- Do some squats while brushing your teeth.
- Add in some exercise to the time you spend doing housework: lunges while using the vacuum cleaner or sweeping, heel raises while dusting, side stretches while cleaning windows.
- Do some exercise following a YouTube video rather than sitting watching mindless television.
- When you first wake in the morning, pause and take some deep breaths. This gets the oxygen flowing to your brain, energising you.
- When you get up in the morning, give some time to do some stretching exercises or arm circles to loosen up the neck and shoulders.
- Run up and down your stairs, gradually increasing your pace from walking gently to running as fast as you can. Do this for five minutes, building up to 10 minutes.
- Go for a walk a with a friend or offer to walk a neighbour's dog.

Top tips for incorporating exercise into your work life:

- Get off public transport a stop earlier and walk in.
- Park your car in a car park further away from your usual parking place or leave your car at home periodically and get public transport to work.
- Don't take the lift – walk up the stairs. To boost fitness, build this up to running. If you push off with your foot flat on the floor rather than on tip-toes you will use your bodyweight to work your muscles more.
- Have a break from a period of very focused work and go out to walk around the building.
- Take a break at lunchtime to eat and go for a walk. A 20 minute mindful walk each day has a positive effect on your productivity. If this isn't possible, try 30 minutes three times a week. If you really want to switch off, listen to some music or a podcast or even learn a language.

Part

2

The body: adrenal health

- Schedule activity in your diary. This is probably the best chance you have of doing it. Set boundaries so you don't replace it with a work demand.
- If your energy feels low during the day, find a quiet spot to do some deep diaphragm breathing – just three deep breaths can energise you.
- If your job is desk-bound, stop periodically and do some simple chair exercises. You could stretch your hands out in front of you, or lean against the backrest with your hands behind your neck, stretching out your elbows, or use the armrest to twist your body to one side then the other.
- Be the one who offers to go out to get hot drinks or water from the cooler.

Activity: Your reflections

Now is the time to reflect on your thoughts and the activities you have completed in the Other Factors affecting Adrenal Health chapter.

Has anything particularly struck you as interesting? Review the chapter in light of the following questions and record your answers below:

- What have you learnt about yourself in this chapter?
- What do you need to change?
- What do you need to start doing that you have not done before?
- What other thoughts do you have?

Part
2

The body: adrenal health

6: How to optimise adrenal function

You may feel you are riding the best wave ever, but it is only sustainable if you regularly come off the wave and get your breath back.

If you're going to prevent burnout, then it's very important that you are honest with yourself and take control in a way that will reverse the effects life's stressors are having on you. If you don't, burnout may well be inevitable.

Be kind to yourself. There is no magic wand I can wave or fairy dust to sprinkle over you that wipes away the pressures and demands of life. You have to find the way yourself to take back control of your life and manage the way you respond to stress.

To keep your adrenals healthy, you will need to make nutritional and lifestyle changes that strengthen you mentally and physically, boosting your capacity to cope naturally so you feel energised, full of vitality and able to perform at optimum capacity. This means making changes that allow you to switch off and return to a normal rhythm of cycling between sympathetic and parasympathetic nervous system mode.

Activity: Your personal perspective on stress

Adrenal health also comes from knowing who you are and what you may be doing that creates the stress in the first place.

Could your personality be the culprit? Are you generating the behaviours that are creating problems for you?

Everyone responds differently to the same triggers, in part because of their individual personality. Identifying which of the four 'stress types' you are will help you decide the most effective steps you can take to help yourself cope.

1. Have a look at the four Personality and Stress Types on the following pages. You will identify which one type most closely describes you. No one type outshines another or is preferable to another; each one has its plus points and its challenges.

2. When you have chosen the type that best describes you, record at the bottom of the chart how you show the characteristics of this type. Add examples of when you have reacted in these ways.

Personality: RESULTS-DRIVEN   Stress Type: OVER-ASSERTIVE

Personality:
- Tough minded, dominating, independent
- Focused and determined
- High energy and attitude
- Know what they want and go out to get it
- Competitive and high achievers; love work
- Like to take charge and be in control of the job and of people
- Goal-focused rather than people-focused
- Good decision makers

Stressors:
- Micro-management
- Incompetence – manager and line reports
- Not delivering on a promise
- Over-emotional responses in others
- Slow pace
- Criticism
- Poorly defined criteria
- Disorganisation
- Lack of recognition for effort and achievements

Symptoms:
- Shows anger
- Becomes domineering
- Becomes inflexible
- Isolates
- Starts to obsess over detail
- Churns previous events over in their head
- Sudden emotional or aggressive outbursts: usually involving 'poor me'

Why you are this type:

Personality: FACTS-DRIVEN   Stress Type: OVER-ANALYTICAL

Personality:
- Focused on thinking and analysis
- All about detail and facts with a good memory for these
- Logical, organised and orderly: likes to be in charge of own schedule
- Task-focused not people-focused
- Values efficiency and consistency
- Prefers routine and tried and tested ways of doing things than the unknown
- Can be critical and detached, or reserved
- Likes a quiet workplace with few interruptions to thinking processes
- Can become obsessive about task in hand
- Suspicious of the future and of creativity

Stressors:
- Unsubstantiated ideas where you have to imagine the outcome
- Winging it with no chance to prepare
- Over-committing so not enough time to give to each item
- Early deadlines without time to provide the detail and do the work justice
- Having to predict the future without evidence
- Unclear direction and instructions
- Lack of accuracy/attention to detail in others' work
- Brainstorming
- Expecting that sense should be made of others' wacky ideas

Symptoms:
- Overdoes the detail and cannot let go - ending up paralysed
- Negative and pessimistic about straightforward matters
- Blames and accuses others
- Anxious with sense of impending doom and disaster
- Fails to listen and misinterprets what others are saying (mind so focused on own thoughts)
- Becomes withdrawn and isolated from others
- Reads meaning into things that are not there
- Loses sleep due to worrying
- Depression
- Eventually becomes inaccurate and unreliable as burnout approaches

Why you are this type:

Personality: RELATIONSHIP-DRIVEN   **Stress Type: OVER-SENSITIVE**

Personality:

- Sociable, approachable, warm
- Dependable and supportive
- Will give, give, give but likes to be appreciated and valued
- Likes harmony and to keep the peace
- Will avoid confrontation and uncomfortable conversations
- Aware of how actions can affect others, reads people well
- Likes to help others whenever possible
- Can express own emotions openly and is comfortable when others do so
- Has strong personal values and convictions and will stick by these
- Likes to feel involved

Stressors:

- A bad atmosphere or conflict
- Controlling, confrontational, critical people
- Highly political environment with 'watch your back' undercurrents
- Unjustified criticism or being undermined or belittled by someone
- Being kept out of the loop
- Being expected to compromise values or personal convictions
- Change – particularly if affecting people
- Too much emphasis on productivity or the bottom line rather than people
- Time pressures that make it difficult to do the job that would please people or match their own expectations of a job well done

Symptoms:

- Compulsive search for answers to why things are this way
- Loss of confidence, so competence suffers
- Becomes more anxious, then judgemental, critical or cynical about self first then about others as stress continues
- Starts to become more cynical and finds fault (e.g. reasons why an idea won't work and should not be supported)
- Acts/talks without concern for how others will feel
- Depression and feelings of helplessness

Why you are this type:

Personality: ATTENTION-DRIVEN

Stress Type: OVER-INDULGENT

Personality:
- Enthusiastic, stimulating, exciting, personable
- Self-aware and people-aware
- Has a vision with good instinct/gut feeling
- Looks to the future with optimism
- Imaginative and creative
- Prefers a flexible approach to work with control over how the work is to be carried out
- Works well with people but prefers autonomy unless someone is fully in-tune with their thinking
- Loves variety and change – hates routine and having to follow delivery through to the end
- Will make their ideas and feelings known

Stressors:
- Having to work with too much detail
- Being expected to follow-through with routine work
- Finding themselves overcommitted so unable to be creative
- Unpredictable demands on their time
- Being micro-managed
- Being mistrusted or having their competence doubted
- Obstinate, irrational people
- Strict rules with prescribed ways of doing the work
- Unchallenging work

Symptoms:
- Feel out of control and overwhelmed
- Starts to anticipate the worst to the extent that things are seen as impossible
- Generally unable to identify the source of the problem
- Begin to internalise physical symptoms (headaches, tummy problems) until they eventually feel they are life-threatening
- Becomes obsessive and over-indulges in food/alcohol/exercise, causing harm to the body
- Sees the world and everyone in it as their enemy
- Insomnia: unable to switch off from problems
- Muscular tension
- Depression, then eventually withdrawal and burnout

Why you are this type:

Part

2

The body: adrenal health

3. As well as helping you to cope with stress better, you could also use these charts to understand other people's behaviour when under stress. This then improves the way you work with them. For example, if a colleague is a 'Results-Driven' type, make sure you always deliver when you promised to.

Personality: RESULTS-DRIVEN
Symptoms: OVER-ASSERTIVE
Solution: WORK WITH OTHERS

- Think logically and prioritise what's important to you and the task
- Talk to someone and get an independent perspective (coach) to clear your head
- Allow others to contribute and help you – don't keep trying to do everything alone
- Learn to listen. Others can help and could have constructive ideas
- Learn to coach others to develop their strengths – this is an investment in your future
- Become more interdependent and less independent
- Stop and take stock of the feelings of others. If you can develop empathy and rapport, colleagues will then work with you rather than against you

Personality: FACTS-DRIVEN
Symptoms: OVER-ANALYTICAL
Solution: MOVE TO ACTION

- Stop and take stock. What is real and what is imagined?
- Stop working to such depth of detail – draw a line, make a decision, and move to action
- Set a deadline to move to action regardless of the state of play
- Consciously get away from it all: go for a pleasurable walk, do some gardening, listen to some music
- Prioritise and allow others to determine what is important
- Delegate more of the detail
- Share your thoughts with a trusted other – ask for help or explore possibilities with them
- Use your logic rather than detail and evidence

Personality: RELATIONSHIPS-DRIVEN
Symptoms: OVER-SENSITIVE
Solution: REFOCUS ON THE POSITIVE

- Stop and take stock. Are you being over-sensitive?
- Refocus on what's going right - not what's going wrong
- Consider the impact of your behaviour on others – are you comfortable with this?
- Try to hide how upset you are – you can't always wear your heart on your sleeve
- Confide in a friend or trusted other that can tell you what's happening
- Take yourself away from it – go for a walk, meditate, or do yoga
- Record your feelings in a journal and reflect on what this means and the impact on yourself and others
- Build a relationship with your line manager so you can elicit honest feedback. Take this as feedback and not criticism
- Ask for help – you offer it to others, so you are also entitled to it

Personality: ATTENTION-DRIVEN
Symptoms: OVER-INDULGENT
Solution: LIGHTEN UP

- Use your creativity to find a different approach. Always look for the opportunity to grow – this will reignite your motivation
- Lighten up – if you're taking things too seriously, you're on your way down. Think logically to get your perspective back
- Allow others to help you with the detail
- Prioritise what you need to do and delegate the follow-through
- Make lists so that you can see what needs to be done, rather than having it all in your head
- Create some space – take some time out to rest, meditate, improve your diet, take light exercise
- Get some coaching as a sounding board to reality
- Encourage feedback

Part

2

The body: adrenal health

Activity: Be kind to yourself

1. Read through the list of suggestions on how you can make changes to your life that will prevent adrenal fatigue.

- **Laugh!** Maintain your humour, and smile whenever you can. Laughter has a powerful impact on the autonomic nervous system, switching you over from sympathetic dominance (doing) to parasympathetic dominance (recovering). Think back to Chapter 3 The Mighty Adrenals where we looked in detail at the workings of the autonomic nervous system. Laughter is a great technique to switch off the 'fight or flight' mechanism and also to shut off adrenal activity.

- **Pace yourself and ease into the day.** Don't just jump out of bed and race to action. Start with taking three deep breaths then spend a few minutes doing some stretching exercises.

- **Set some non-negotiable boundaries** between your professional life and your personal life. For example, you do not have to be a slave to your email and phone.

- **Schedule time for recovery.** Have at least 15 minutes in the day that you devote completely to you, doing nothing. Blank out time in your diary if necessary.

- **Treat yourself to something that refreshes you.** Don't feel guilty: it's an essential part of restoring balance. Have a massage, try a relaxing bath or even start a new hobby… anything that distracts you from the tension and strain that is building in your life.

- **Reflect on the challenges you may be experiencing.** Why are they a challenge, how are you reacting, what effect is this having on you, and how can you change the situation?

- **Take time to check in.** Ask yourself the following and consider what your answers are telling you. What do you realise that you are addicted to? What are your energy levels like? What are your memory and concentration like? How are you reacting to the pressures you're experiencing? How are you interacting with others? How happy are you? Where have you lost balance in your life?

- **Forgive yourself for any problems and mistakes.** It's a new day and a new start tomorrow. What is past has gone.

- **Have an annual MOT.** Ask your doctor to check your blood pressure and do some blood tests. These should include fasting blood sugar, cholesterol and thyroid.

- **Know your life priorities.** What are you passionate about? Write down the most important things in your life (professional and personal) and pin them up somewhere you will see them frequently and regularly. Measure whether you are living your passions and consider how you will avoid compromising them. They are your rock and your lifeline to a balanced life.

- **Be sociable.** As tempting as it might be when you're struggling to cope, don't isolate yourself.

- **Speak up.** Don't be ashamed if you are finding it hard to cope right now. Talk to someone close to you – a family member or friend. Better still, talk to your manager, but if your manager is the problem, speak to HR or occupational health, or utilise your company's Employee Assistance Programme counselling contract if they have one. It's a free, confidential service that allows you to talk about anything from financial worries to child care issues as well as stress-related problems.

Part
2

The body: adrenal health

- **Take a break.** Use your holiday entitlement and have some time off. Before you go, write a big to-do list covering everything outstanding for you to do on your return. Brief your team on any anticipated problems and what to do in your absence. Choose somewhere relaxing and switch off all your digital technology. Delegate someone to cover phone and email messages whilst away, or put on an autoresponder.

  If you really have to check into the office, set aside a time to do this each day/every other day, for example, for one hour each morning at 10am, before you go to sit by the pool. Be strict and tell people this is the only time you will be available.

- **If you need it, take time out.** If you're getting close to burnout, it's important you take some time out and have a complete break, with no work interruptions. This may require a discussion with your manager, HR or occupational health. It is becoming a more common occurrence so don't feel embarrassed, ashamed or cross with yourself. You have not failed – it's because you have done so much that you're in this situation. Turn your life around and use your experience to learn, change and grow.

- **Get help.** If things have gone too far, then get help; you cannot solve the problem alone at this stage. See your doctor. Do you need time off or maybe referral for Cognitive Behavioural Therapy (CBT)?

2. What will you do? When will you start? How will you make things
   work better for you? What support do you need to help you?
   Record your answers here.

Activity: The power of breath

Breathing is a powerful way to relax you and switch off the sympathetic nervous system.

Try the following exercise:

1. Sit comfortably on a chair (not a bed or you will fall asleep – unless you want to do this).

2. Think about how you feel sitting on the chair. Where are your feet placed and how do they feel? What about your buttocks on the seat of the chair? How does your back feel against the chair? How are your shoulders feeling, and your head and neck on your shoulders?

3. Now concentrate on your breathing. Where are you breathing? In the shallow upper part of your chest or deep into your belly?

4. Place your hand on your belly, relax your jaw then take a deep breath in through your nose for the count of four. You should notice your belly rise up. If it's difficult to breathe through your nose, breathe through your mouth.

5. As soon as the breath finishes, breathe out for the count of eight and notice your hands fall. As you reach the end of the breath, pull your stomach back towards your spine. This will allow you to exhale the last bit of air.

6. Continue with deep belly breaths, focusing your mind on the inhale and exhale in rhythmic movement, with the out breath lasting twice as long as the in breath. If you find it difficult to think of your breath, think about a wave coming into the shore then out again.

7. Do this for about two minutes. Then return to gentle breathing.

8. Repeat this exercise every evening when you arrive home from work.

Activity: Your reflections

Now is the time to reflect on your thoughts and the activities you have completed in the How to Optimise Adrenal Function chapter.

Has anything particularly struck you as interesting? Review the chapter in light of the following questions and record your answers below:

- What have you learnt about yourself in this chapter?
- What do you need to change?
- What do you need to start doing that you have not done before?
- What other thoughts do you have?

Part

2

The body: adrenal health

Part 3
The mind:
healthy attitudes

7: What is an attitude? The Burnout Attitude Model

We do not see with our eyes; we see with our brains!

An attitude is your version of a situation based on what you think, believe and feel about something. It's how you see yourself and the world; it's your mindset.

It is a pretty settled way of thinking, based on the evaluation you make of your experiences, beliefs, feelings and values. Your attitude then shapes the

143

way you subsequently behave. Attitudes are completely individual and can only be formed by you.

They are hidden away in your subconscious mind and you basically let them get on with it, working away automatically below the surface. It is only when faced with a new event or situation or something that is not as it should be that you switch to conscious mode and give any thought to what your attitudes may actually mean.

Attitudes can be positive or negative. They have enormous power. They can empower you or limit you, because what you think and tell yourself, you will do.

If you tell yourself you are brave, then you are less likely to be fearful. If you tell yourself you have done well, you will feel more confident the next time you're faced with that situation.

Switch off your autopilot and take control

A 24/7, always on, highly demanding lifestyle means that not only is life, whether it be work or personal, placing demands on you, but that your own attitudes may well be making an already challenging situation even worse. You therefore need to switch off autopilot and take control of your attitudes, particularly if they are negatively affecting your wellbeing. Although attitudes are relatively enduring and therefore hard to change, the good news is that if an attitude is limiting us, you can change it.

Persistence is key. By working on the new attitude many times, you will eventually learn to think that way automatically.

144

Case study

Claire was a highly aspirational Young Professional who knew exactly where she wanted her career to go. She was thankful that she worked for such a great company; a leader in the market which paid well and provided opportunities for promotion.

Claire worked very hard. It was tough, but she saw it as an investment in her future success. As well as the hours being long (at least ten hour days in the office), she also had to check emails at home in case a client had been in touch. This meant firing up her laptop on a Sunday afternoon to get on top of things before the start of another busy week.

She was keen to get noticed so she was extra diligent in checking that work never went out to her manager or a client with a mistake. She knew this added to her workload, but it was worth it to avoid those ghastly feelings she experienced when something did go wrong. Then she'd beat herself up for days, which was a distraction she could do without.

The long days were hard on her social life, leaving very little time to see friends and family. It had got worse recently because she was feeling so tired and not sleeping too well, so when she wasn't working, she found she just wanted to sleep.

Claire felt strongly that if you want to get on in this world, you have to get on well with people. She always tried to give people time, helping them if they needed it; she was empathic to their opinions and tried to take these on board whenever she had an important decision to make. People were always nice to her in return and she felt they appreciated the help she gave them, even if she was asked to do something that didn't necessarily relate to her tasks.

Then came the day that changed everything for Claire. She'd had a busy morning preparing for an important meeting she was attending shortly after lunch. There had been quite a few interruptions to her planned morning, including a tricky problem she had to sort out with a client. She hadn't got as far as she'd hoped.

Claire got up from her desk to go to the photocopier and as she was leaving the room, one of her colleagues said to her that if she was going to do some copying, could she just do these couple of things for her? Claire froze, her mind kept saying time, time, time.... and with that, she collapsed to the floor.

This minor incident was the straw that broke the camel's back. Claire had burnt out.

This is a true story. Claire was off work for six months. She couldn't bear to even think about work. On the day she was due to return, she found she just couldn't do it – the very thought of all that work was too much for her to bear. The very career that Claire had valued so much had gone.

What had happened to Claire? She was focused and aspirational but her attitudes to what would have accelerated her career were not particularly healthy. She didn't know when to stop and she didn't understand the warning signs.

What about you? Read on. This section will develop the concept of healthy attitudes further.

Activity: Your attitudes questionnaire

Attitudes heavily influence what you subsequently think and do. It's important to know how your attitudes may be affecting you. Try this questionnaire.

1. Read the statements below and, thinking about yourself over the last three months, consider how much you agree with each statement.

2. Circle the number that most closely reflects your answer where:

1 = Strongly disagree
2 = Disagree
3 = No strong feelings either way
4 = Agree
5 = Strongly agree

What's my attitude?					
1 I am competitive with a constant need for achievement	1	2	3	4	5
2 I have high standards	1	2	3	4	5
3 I prefer to do the job myself. That way I can ensure it gets done properly	1	2	3	4	5
4 I think it's safer to be more pessimistic than optimistic	1	2	3	4	5
5 I have a voice inside my head always on alert to judge me	1	2	3	4	5
6 I get more done by being on my own	1	2	3	4	5
7 I cannot say 'No' to anyone's request for help	1	2	3	4	5
8 I like to have a number of tasks on the go simultaneously	1	2	3	4	5
9 I get distressed when I submit work with a mistake	1	2	3	4	5
10 I am always on alert to critique and correct other people's work	1	2	3	4	5
11 I focus on the things that can and have gone wrong	1	2	3	4	5
12 When I've made a mistake I find it hard to switch off seeing where I went wrong	1	2	3	4	5

Part
3

The mind: healthy attitudes

13	I prefer not to talk or engage with my colleagues, in case they expect something from me	1	2	3	4	5
14	I feel guilty saying 'No'; I'd hate to think I let someone down	1	2	3	4	5
15	I must always be accessible so I frequently check my phone and computer for messages	1	2	3	4	5
16	I regularly check my work to improve it	1	2	3	4	5
17	I am obliged to tell people what they should do, so that they work effectively	1	2	3	4	5
18	I find it difficult to see the funny side of life	1	2	3	4	5
19	I blame myself when something fails, even if it's a team effort	1	2	3	4	5
20	I am focused on my work so have little time for socialising	1	2	3	4	5
21	I feel obliged to help people senior to me no matter how busy I am	1	2	3	4	5
22	I feel guilty relaxing	1	2	3	4	5
23	I avoid situations where the outcome might not be perfect	1	2	3	4	5
24	I produce more than my co-workers do and to a better standard	1	2	3	4	5

25	I focus more on what's bad in my job rather than what's good	1	2	3	4	5
26	I place more emphasis on my weaknesses, ignoring my strengths	1	2	3	4	5
27	I don't have the time for interests and hobbies outside of work	1	2	3	4	5
28	I am not skilled at being assertive	1	2	3	4	5
29	I am my work; it defines who I am	1	2	3	4	5
30	I like my surroundings to be organised so I can find things easily	1	2	3	4	5
31	I am better working independently so I can decide how things are done	1	2	3	4	5
32	I assume things are hopeless first, before I try them	1	2	3	4	5
33	I feel worthless	1	2	3	4	5
34	I do not have the capacity to listen to other people's problems right now	1	2	3	4	5
35	I feel put-upon because people abuse my generosity	1	2	3	4	5

Part

3

The mind: healthy attitudes

Scoring chart

Now transpose your answers onto the scoring chart below.

1. Each box relates to a question. The box numbered 1 relates to
    Question 1 so put your score for Question 1 in that box. The
    box with number 2 is for your answer to Question 2 and so on.

2. Add up each row and put the score in the final
    right-hand column.

Extreme Driver	1	8	15	22	29	
Perfectionist	2	9	16	23	30	
Control Freak	3	10	17	24	31	
Negative Thinker	4	11	18	25	32	
Inner Critic	5	12	19	26	33	

Social Isolator	6	13	20	27	34	
People Pleaser	7	14	21	28	35	

The Burnout Attitude Model
©Susan Scott 2016

The Burnout Attitude Model is composed of seven different attitudes. Each of these attitudes stimulates a stress response, contributing to burnout in its own way.

Each of these attitudes is listed in the Scoring Chart above. Look at your score for each element.

1. If you scored 10 or less for an attitude, then it is likely that you do not possess this attitude in a way that could contribute to burnout.

2. If you scored 15 or more, then it is likely that this attitude may be adding internal demands that could lead you to burnout.

3. Look at the definition of each element below, then turn to the relevant pages where you can find out more about these attitudes together with exercises on how to manage them to minimise the risks they pose.

Bear in mind that there's often some overlap between these attitudes, so you may well find it helpful to read about all of them.

Extreme Drivers are highly driven to achieve, pushing themselves to the limits to get noticed and promoted. They define themselves by their work, so they find it hard to switch off from it.

Perfectionists have a set of distorted beliefs and rules that drive them to put pressure on themselves to achieve unrealistically high standards.

Control Freaks are people with a strong desire to exert control over people and situations. They believe that things should be done right and perfectly and only they know how to achieve this.

Negative Thinkers have a subconscious, irrational thought process that looks to the bad and discounts the good.

Inner Critics have a self-defeating voice inside their heads that judges and criticises all aspects of how they think and behave, leaving them with a sense that they are not good enough.

Social Isolators believe that the only way to get the job done is to separate themselves as much as possible from colleagues, family and close friends.

People Pleasers have an attitude that there will be consequences if they say 'No' to someone's request for assistance.

Activity: Your reflections

It is time again to reflect on your thoughts and the results of Your Attitudes Questionnaire you completed above.

- What have you learnt about yourself?
- What do you need to change?
- What do you need to start doing that you have not done before?
- What other thoughts do you have?

Part

3

The mind: healthy attitudes

This section will now develop each of the seven attitudes further. Read all seven, but pay special attention to the ones for which you scored fifteen or more, and complete the exercises.

8: Extreme driver

- Are you competitive with a constant need for achievement?
- Do you like to have a number of tasks on the go simultaneously?
- Do you feel guilty relaxing?
- Do you over-identify with your work - it defines who you are?
- Are you always accessible, frequently checking your phone and computer for messages?

If you answered Yes to any of these questions, you could be an Extreme Driver.

Case study

Charlie worked in sales for a software developer. He was driven and ambitious and believed that to prove his potential, he needed to exceed his targets. He identified an opportunity for a big sale.

Having this plus the other leads he was working on recently meant he was now working pretty much seven days a week – but if everything went well, he would

155

smash his target for this quarter and really reap the benefits financially. This excited Charlie.

Charlie had a strong belief that you should 'get on and do your work' and didn't have much time for chit chat when in the office. He also didn't share much about himself or ask many questions. He was feeling very confident, so when his manager or colleagues in the team asked how things were going, he'd say things were good and under control.

He thought it odd that people kept asking how he was doing; they didn't normally show such care. He was also surprised when he'd told his mother one weekend that he might not be able to make it to his dad's big birthday party and she was cross with him – it was just a birthday.

The day came to present to the client's board and there were a few tricky questions in the Q&A, particularly from the Financial Director who wanted certain details on costings. But he felt he managed to gloss over them. It came as quite a bombshell when the customer chose another supplier. The reason they gave was that they didn't feel Charlie was being open enough with them over... costs.

Charlie was putting his ambitions ahead of reality and it was clouding his judgement. It became all about work, but he was taking this to an extreme and therefore he came unstuck.

Drive has to be balanced with recovery. When you're an Extreme Driver, you have to give yourself permission to pause. The mind needs time to rest and reflect. If you allow it that, it will work away subconsciously, helping you achieve what you have aspired to do.

The fact that Charlie's manager and colleagues were asking how he was, was an indicator that Charlie was overdoing it and wasn't coping as well as he thought. Charlie had become snappy and was easily irritated with people. He'd started smoking again, something he gave up when he finished university. He was very impatient – time was money, so get a move on! Charlie was stuck in overdrive, without much rational and logical thinking.

Looking back, Charlie now believes that losing this contract saved him from spiralling into collapse.

What is an Extreme Driver?

Extreme Drivers have a mindset that is all about doing and achieving. They are highly driven to achieve, pushing themselves to the limits to get noticed and promoted. Extreme Drivers are defined by their work so they find it hard to switch off. As there are only so many hours in the day, something else has to give, and that will usually be their personal life and their relaxation time.

The arrival of the digital age has meant 24/7 access to work and information makes it even easier for the Extreme Driver to be a workaholic. Technology is addictive to Extreme Drivers. It provides the means to be always accessible and it makes everything and everyone accessible to them. It fills every moment of their time if they let it, even though Information Technology is only really there as a tool to help you do your job, not dominate your job and your life.

How can being an Extreme Driver burn you out?

If you are an Extreme Driver, take note; the reality is that the road to burnout is paved with good intentions.

Whilst being highly driven, self-motivated and hard-working might be good for your employer and your career, working long hours, giving every spare moment to 'doing' without taking time to recharge and recover, eventually will have consequences – and that can affect more than your energy. You'll miss out on the 'special' things in life that don't involve work but involve relationships with family and friends, as well as special experiences. Above all, being a workaholic is only sustainable for so long before it affects health, sleep, productivity, creativity, mental health and relationships – it's the fastest route to burnout.

To prevent burnout, Extreme Drivers need to create a healthier balance with defined boundaries between work and home and must prevent these from becoming blurred. This is a big ask, but essential.

Over-engaging with your work without recovery diminishes wellbeing – it's as simple and as fundamental as that.

As an Extreme Driver, it is far better for you to ensure that your level of work engagement is balanced with non-work activities that allow for physical and mental rejuvenation. Not only do you recover, but this widens your horizons, makes you happier and more productive and grows your overall wellbeing.

Part

3

The mind: healthy attitudes

157

Achieving this happy balance starts with understanding why you are so driven – what you are so keen to achieve. From here you can begin to identify the most important things in your whole life – obviously your work, but also what your personal priorities are. Then finally, consider how you can balance these.

You can still be a high achiever, but this way you will have the energy to make it sustainable.

Activity: Your ideal life

The purpose of this exercise is to take off your blinkers, to see your life as a whole and to identify what is important to you. The idea is to put your whole life into perspective, not just the part you define by work.

It is important that you answer the questions from your own perspective; not adopt someone else's or that of your employer. This is your perspective on your life.

- Why are you so driven? What do you want to achieve from your life?
  a. Describe what you want to achieve from life. What gives you a sense of purpose and meaning?

- What are the things that are most important to you in your life – the things you value most? Think about work, family, friends, career, hobbies, interests and spiritual matters.
  a. Do these values relate to work or non-work? What is the percentage balance between your work and non-work values, e.g. 80% work values and 20% non-work values?

- What is the current situation?
  a. Ask yourself – how close are you to your ideal life? On a scale of 1 to 10, where 1 is "nowhere close' and 10 is 'I'm there', how close are you to living a life embracing all the things you value most?

Nowhere close							I'm there		
1	2	3	4	5	6	7	8	9	10

b. What are the top 5 things you value most in your life? Record your answers in the box below.

Value 1	
Value 2	
Value 3	
Value 4	
Value 5	

c. Why is each value so important to you?

Value 1	
Value 2	

Part 3

The mind: healthy attitudes

Value 3	
Value 4	
Value 5	

d. Where are you in terms of living each value? What is the balance like between the things you value most in your life? How much time do you allow for the things you value most in your life?

Value 1	
Value 2	

Value 3	
Value 4	
Value 5	

e. If where you are today does not match with where you would like to be, what are you losing out on?

f. To what degree has the current situation been determined by you or by someone or something else?

- What needs to change?
  a. Considering the things you value most, how will you allow them into your life?

b. How can you realistically balance this with your work? Who can help you do this?

Now ensure you spend time doing the things that are important to you in your life. Work can be draining, but outside work activities and relationships are energising, providing you with the opportunity to recharge so that you actually do a better job in the long run.

Activity: How do you spend your time?

Extreme Drivers prioritise work over personal life. But if you bring work home, how much time do you really spend at home? Consider and complete the following:

Activity	Hours: Work time	Hours: Home time
Sleep		
Washing, dressing, undressing		
Food shopping, cooking, eating, clearing up		
Housework, home maintenance		
Children		
Commuting		
Meetings		
Emails		
Work phone calls		
Face-to-face conversations		
Work administration		
Writing reports		
Presentations		
Managing staff		
Other work travel		
Sport, exercise		
Reading, listening to music		
Personal phone calls		
Socialising		

Part

3

The mind: healthy attitudes

Watch carefully for the blurring of boundaries, shown in actions such as handling work emails and work phone calls at home, showering at the office, work travel at the weekend or on a day off or going to the gym during a work day.

You can still be driven to achieve, but it is important to take the time to switch off and do something else. Ask yourself the following:

1. Looking at this chart, what do you see?
2. How many hours are you really working?
3. Are there defined boundaries between work and home?
4. What are you doing at home that's really an activity for the office?
5. What are you doing at the office that you should be doing at home?
6. How can you strengthen the boundaries between work and home?
7. Where could you fit in more of the things you really value in life?
8. Are you allowing enough time for recovery? Look at the top tips below for ideas.

Top tips for changing Extreme Driver attitudes:

- **Schedule your whole life into your diary,** not just your work life. Know the things that will always take priority and cannot be changed. This goes just as much for personal activities as work activities.

- **Manage digital technology** – it's a big distraction to getting your job done. You need to take control of emails by making rules that allow you to control it, not the other way around.

  - Ensure your email is not set-up to automatically receive and notify you. This prevents you from being interrupted and eliminates the temptation to check it constantly
  - Schedule specific times to check and respond to emails. Choose 'low productivity' time to do this – remember there are certain times of day when you probably do your best work, so do not use this time to email

- Turn emails into actions. If an email will take more than a few minutes to action or respond to, add it as a new action on your To-Do List
- Bring in some email rules in your team. Discourage people from writing essays. Where possible, limit emails to a paragraph or sentence. Ensure the subject header reflects the conversation so you know whether to read the email. Discourage people from using the 'reply to all' button unless it's necessary
- Use rules in the email system to automatically divert emails on non-urgent topics to folders you set up e.g. newsletters, hobbies, training
- Set a time deadline on using email at home. Have a cut off time after which you no longer respond to emails. Just because your client sends them at 10pm doesn't mean you have to respond then

- **Take regular breaks.** The body and mind work to a rhythm of activity and rest. In every hour, work for fifty minutes with concerted effort and concentration, then spend ten minutes doing something completely different. This recharges your attention, making you fit again for more focused attention.

- **Know when you've reached saturation.** Take time out – go for a walk at lunchtime, or do some stretching exercises, listen to calming music, read an extract from an inspiring book, go to a café for a drink. You will be much more productive when you return to your desk and less likely to have to bring work home.

- **Do something restorative.** Are short interludes in a busy day enough or do you need something longer, perhaps taking a long weekend away with the family?

- **Learn to switch off.** It doesn't come easily when you're always in 'doing' mode. Make time to do and think about something other than work in the evenings and at the weekend.

Prioritisation is a skill – learn it.

Part
3

The mind: healthy attitudes

Activity: What are your priorities?

The reality is that you cannot always do it all. Prioritisation is a skill that allows you to manage the chaos of excessive, competing demands on your time, and focus on the most important and urgent activities. In other words, you allocate your time to where it's most needed.

1. Write a to-do list. Record everything you need to do, from today for one week.
2. What are the deadlines for these activities?
3. What is their priority? This is based on what is the most urgent and important to YOU (not someone else's urgent and important). Allocate a priority by scoring each activity from one to five where one is the highest priority and five is the lowest.

Activity	Deadline	Priority (1-5)

Now look at your to-do list. How achievable is this during work hours? How realistic are your deadlines? What is and is not in your power to do?

What do you need to do to achieve your demands in work hours? Do you need assistance or could you delegate some tasks?

When you arrive for work each morning, do not fire up your computer and hit your email straight away. Always deal with the highest or trickiest priority first, otherwise you'll be sucked in, your to-do list will be side-lined and you'll never accomplish anything of importance.

Activity: Your reflections

What has resonated with you while reading about the Extreme Driver attitude?

- What have you learnt about yourself?
- What do you need to change?
- What do you need to start doing that you have not done before?
- What other thoughts do you have?

9: Perfectionist

- Do you have high standards?
- Do you spend excessive amounts of time checking and improving your work?
- Does it devastate you when you discover that you submitted some work with a mistake?
- Do you avoid situations if you're unsure that the outcome will be perfect?
- Do you like things to be organised so you can find them easily?
- Do you tend to take criticism personally?
- Does it concern you that people might think badly of you?

If you answered Yes to any of these questions, you could be a Perfectionist.

Case study

Sam worked in marketing for a consultancy. He had some big names as clients. One of Sam's projects required him to write a marketing brochure. He wrote it but didn't like it, so he rewrote it. On his long journey home each evening, he would give time to thinking what he could do to make it just right and when he got home he'd tweak it again.

The closer it got to the deadline for completing it and sending it to the client, the more he worked on it, but it never felt perfect and this was really playing on his mind and stressing him. On the day of the deadline, he showed his manager what he had developed, apologised and shared his worries that it wasn't good enough. His manager had some wise words:

"Sam – whether you think it's good or not, it is way better than anything the client can do – so send it. Why didn't you come to me earlier?" Sam had created anxiety for no good reason other than it had to be absolutely perfect, even though no one had told him so.

Sam's problem was that he always felt unprepared. He had very high standards and nothing was quite good enough. Trying to make everything perfect took up valuable time when he could have been doing something else, like recovering. His expectations of 'perfect' were unrealistic: nothing is truly perfect.

This early lesson taught him to share his thoughts more and find out what others expected of him. That way he could deliver to that expectation, not what his perfectionist mindset told him, which saved him a lot of time – and bucket loads of anxiety.

What is a Perfectionist?

Perfectionists have a set of distorted beliefs and rules that drive them to put pressure on themselves to achieve unrealistically high standards. These self-determined thoughts, even though they may never have been proposed or endorsed by their manager, employer or family, convince them that it is only by reaching these standards that people will think well of them and provide them with opportunities for recognition and advancement.

Perfectionists judge themselves on the quality of everything they do. This critiquing has a powerful impact on their fragile self-esteem, (sense of self-worth and how they value themselves) and self-confidence, affecting their mental, as well as physical, wellbeing.

How can being a Perfectionist burn you out?

If you have a Perfectionist attitude, you risk burnout because you do everything you can to make things perfect and prevent mistakes from occurring.

You set rigid rules to work by, checking work repeatedly and writing copious lists, all of which take up precious time and energy. You may also avoid everything and anything that might put you at risk of failure, such as not offering up ideas unless you can back them up with something smart, or taking on a new task if you're not familiar with it because it may expose you.

While Perfectionists pride themselves on creating the very best work, to others they can appear to be anxious, rigid, inflexible procrastinators who won't start something new unless they're sure they're going to be successful at it.

A Perfectionist is never satisfied and will therefore set ever higher standards. Whereas once the standards were easy to achieve and you were complimented and rewarded, in time, as you set the bar ever-higher, they become more difficult to live up to, and you start to make mistakes.

Setting higher standards is a good thing if they're realistic and you use the learning to improve and grow in capability. But when you are over-critical, view even the smallest mistake as a failure and obsess about it, as Perfectionists do, then this unhealthy attitude drains your energy and time and becomes self-destructive.

The reality is that true perfection is unachievable, so trying to achieve it is a waste of precious energy. You can only do the best you can. You gain nothing but lose a lot if you're too hard on yourself.

Perfectionists are hard to manage, hard to work with and create a very hard life for those managed by them. They not only have high standards for themselves, but everyone else. Is this what you really want to be known as?

The starting point is to identify how you distort reality, and why you have this belief. Once this is done, you can put in countermeasures to change these self-defeating attitudes.

Part
3

The mind: healthy attitudes

Activity: What is your Perfectionist mindset?

It is the personal beliefs and attitudes stored away in your subconscious mind that result in your Perfectionist behaviour. This exercise is designed to tap into your subconscious and highlight how and why you have formed these attitudes.

Is it your past experiences, or down to the things you value the most? Is it because you like people to recognise you for being the best, or is it as simple as feeling that it's just better to get things absolutely right the first time you do them?

1. What are your Perfectionist beliefs?

   a. What are the things you believe you must/mustn't, should/shouldn't, can/can't do?
   b. Why do you think this way? Who told you? Where have you seen it?
   c. How do you judge how well you uphold your Perfectionist beliefs?
   d. How flexible are you on these beliefs?
   e. Are these beliefs in just one section of your life or across all parts of your life?

Beliefs I must/mustn't, should/shouldn't, can/can't….	**Why you think this way**

2. What are your Perfectionist behaviours?

   a. Tick the behaviours that apply to you. Add more if you notice a behaviour that is not listed.

   b. Next to each behaviour you have ticked, write why you do this and how it makes you feel.

Behaviour	√	Why do I do this? How does it make me feel?
Sets very high standards and does everything possible to achieve them with no mistakes		
Expects very high standards of others and can become critical if they have not been met		
Can be very self-critical which impacts self-esteem		

Behaviour	√	Why do I do this? How does it make me feel?
Fears getting things wrong, so avoids things that can't be done perfectly		
Takes mistakes personally. Sees them as a failure and finds it hard to move on from them		
Can blow things out of proportion and becomes emotional when a mistake is made		
Gets consumed by internal chatter, finding it hard to switch off when there has been a mistake		
Likes to be organised and tidy		
Excessive list making – lists for everything!		

Behaviour	√	Why do I do this? How does it make me feel?
Has a keen eye for detail		
Takes each task seriously, but may have difficulty prioritising them		
Likes to be recognised for being competent and delivering to a high standard		
Does not handle criticism well, taking it very personally		
Will work on a number of iterations of a piece of work to get the best possible, even if perfection is not required. Doesn't know when to say enough is enough.		
Always checks work for mistakes		

Part

3

The mind: healthy attitudes

Behaviour	√	Why do I do this? How does it make me feel?
Worries that vital information is missing that would make the work even better		
Procrastinates if you feel you don't have all the information available		
Takes work home so you have a more peaceful environment to think straight the next day		
Dislikes taking risks in case it fails		
Concerned by what others may think and whether they'll think badly of you		
Finds it difficult to make decisions in case it's the wrong one		

4. What are the benefits of being a Perfectionist? Consider this both professionally and personally.

5. What are the disadvantages – the consequences for you.

Benefits of perfectionism	Disadvantages of perfectionism

6. What Perfectionist beliefs and behaviours could you relax? It's about 'lightening up', not completely changing or compromising your standards. The aim is to reduce stress and anxiety levels so that you still perform, but in a way that prevents burnout.

Top tips for changing Perfectionist attitudes:

- **Don't fear mistakes.** Instead, give yourself permission to make a mistake. Mistakes are an inherent part of being human. Ask yourself: how much will this matter next month?

- **Think about the 80:20 rule.** Getting things right 100% of the time is unrealistic. It's much healthier to work towards it 80% of the time.

- **Be kinder to yourself.** Forgive yourself. There is no such thing as perfection – things could always be better. Congratulate yourself on the job you did.

Part
3

The mind: healthy attitudes

- **Accept that life is for learning.** Admit to yourself that you don't know everything. Asking for help is not a sign of weakness or failure, and you will be more successful when you interact with others.

- **View criticism as helpful feedback** and identify what you could learn from it.

- **Set a limit on checking.** Be firm with yourself and recognise when enough is enough. If you find that you keep checking your work for mistakes, set yourself a time limit. All you're doing is wasting time and energy correcting something that's already good enough.

- **Focus on the bigger picture.** When you focus your attention on just one thing, such as a spelling mistake, it means you've gone into tunnel vision and that isn't good for your wellbeing.

- **Tune into your self-talk.** If you find yourself getting anxious, frustrated or unhappy, tune into what you are telling yourself you must/mustn't, should/shouldn't do. Now assess how realistic these expectations are. It may be better to lower the bar.

- **Praise yourself.** Don't rely on others to praise you – that's too big an ask when people are struggling with the demands of their own lives. Regularly congratulate and praise yourself. Record your praises in a diary.

- **Practice your new behaviour.** It can be very hard to change when you're a Perfectionist, so record here why you are doing this. You may have to remind yourself from time to time.

Why I am changing my Perfectionist beliefs and behaviours.

Activity: What are your strengths and weaknesses?

1. What do you do well?
2. What do you not do so well?

Look at your everyday activities inside and outside work. What you do well may be things you do routinely without much thought because you are so skilled. Don't dismiss them.

Maybe you have overcome a difficult situation; what helped you to overcome it? Things you don't do so well may be the things you avoid doing or the areas in which you make mistakes.

What I do well	What I don't do so well

Part 3

The mind: healthy attitudes

Whenever you're about to beat yourself up, look at this chart. Perhaps you've made a mistake – no matter how big or small – or maybe you've forgotten something important. Rather than letting the error dominate your thinking, tell yourself, "I might have made this mistake, but look how well I used my skills".

Activity: Your reflections

What has resonated with you while reading about the Perfectionist attitude?

- What have you learnt about yourself?
- What do you need to change?
- What do you need to start doing that you have not done before?
- What other thoughts do you have?

10: Control freak

- Do you prefer to do the job yourself, because that way you can ensure it gets done properly?
- Are you always on alert to critique and correct other people's work?
- Do you feel obliged to tell people what they should do, so they work effectively?
- Do you believe that things get done better when you take charge?
- Do you find it difficult to delegate?
- Do you distrust other people's judgement and prefer to take decisions yourself?
- Do you like people to listen to what you have to say?
- Do you prefer to work independently so you can decide how things are done?

If you answered Yes to any of these questions, you could be a Control Freak.

Case study

Luke was offered an opportunity to go on secondment within his firm to lead a new strategic project. Luke was sure he'd been chosen because he was so adept at delivering well and on time. He had a team of six.

They had a variety of skills but weren't quite the finished article in his opinion. In his mind, this meant he would have to take tight control of this team if it was going to achieve the best outcome.

Luke spent six months forcing staff to work the way he worked. He even went so far as to make tracked changes to documents they had written. He frequently took over work that they had been assigned to do because it became easier to do it himself than explain what to do – plus he knew it was done properly then. He was ok with this as it meant it would show them the way the work should be done.

For a couple of weeks, it worked. But then the open warfare began. There were arguments, one person blatantly ignored him, others did their basic work-hours but not one hour more, and this was far from helpful when there was so much to do. On top of everything else, he now had to manage 'their antics' as well as the tasks themselves, which meant he was working longer and longer hours. Luke was struggling to cope, and one day, standing on the train on his way into the office, he fainted.

Luke had found it hard to let go. He believed he was the only one who knew how to do it properly yet the reality was he was working with a team whose members had been chosen because they were intelligent, sensible and capable. His lack of trust in people overloaded him and cheesed off everyone around him into the bargain, adding even more work.

Luke had a lot on his plate, but much of the overload was self-inflicted. If he was going to stop it affecting his health, then he needed to find a way to step back.

What is a Control Freak?

Control Freak is an attitude that if the job is going to be done properly, then you must either do it yourself or must exert control over other people and situations to get the job done.

The Control Freak mindset is one that tells you that you are the only one who knows how to do something. Control Freaks fear allowing another person to do anything without constant supervision. So, when tasks do need to be done by others, the Control Freak will become directive, critiquing and instructing on every aspect.

Because in their eyes they do the job well, Control Freaks find it hard to recognise that they're doing anything wrong. Not only are they unnecessarily overloading themselves, the reality is, they can't control everything and by failing to let go, they're treating others unfairly. They lose sight of the fact that everyone has their own way of achieving something and there's every chance that it could be done equally well someone else's way.

By failing to delegate, and stifling free thinking, they obstruct opportunities for others to learn and develop. This is self-defeating because it prevents people from learning and taking on additional responsibilities. It also means that the Control Freak never gets to free themselves of some of their responsibilities.

How can being a Control Freak burn you out?

Beware! A Control Freak attitude means that you'll eventually run yourself into the ground trying to do everything. Instead, you need to let go and delegate.

Relinquishing control generates more success when others develop and grow in confidence – that's the power of joint effort. It begins with changing some of the beliefs that make you think you need to do everything yourself because no one else is as capable as you.

Start to think of achieving results as a joint effort. There may be times when you do need to take control and be directive; there are also times when you really are the best person to do the job. But likewise, there are times when the other person is perfectly capable of achieving the desired results without your directive approach, and you could even learn something from this!

As a Control Freak you need to lighten up, release the chains and adopt a more flexible approach to getting the job done. This is summarised in the following diagram.

Part

3

The mind: healthy attitudes

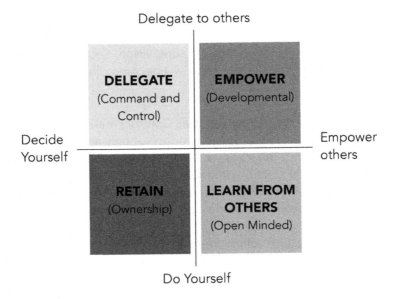

The Working Effectively With Others Model
©Susan Scott 2016

If you are a Control Freak, to prevent this attitude from burning you out, you need to control the way you work in a more flexible manner.
Let's look at this in more detail:

Retain: This is where you decide what to do and do it yourself. You keep full ownership, responsibility and authority to deliver yourself.

Delegate: This is where you make the decisions but then delegate the action to another to complete. It's about being directive.

Empower: This is where you trust and allow another to decide how the job is to be done and allow them to carry it out their way. They take responsibility and have full authority.

Learn from Others: This is about being open-minded to other possible ways of achieving the required results. You see and learn from others.

Rather than believing you have to control everything, try positioning yourself in Delegate or Empower from time to time. You will do far better when you apply all four activities when working with and managing people.

Activity: What do you have to control?

To lighten up on controlling others, you need to open your mind to the fact that there are other ways of doing things. You never know, you may learn something new!

Consider the following:

1. What do you actually have authority to control?
2. How much control do others have over you?
3. What situations and people do you try to control?
4. What do you take control of that others should be delivering?
5. How would you feel if someone were controlling you when you knew you were capable?

Activity: Control mode

Having a Control Freak attitude happens instinctively, typically without conscious thought. In order to change, you need to evaluate the situation consciously, and identify why you believe it is necessary to take control. Yes, taking control may be justified, but if it's not, then you need to change your attitude. Try this exercise:

1. Think of a situation you believe you should control.
2. Why do you think you need to take control – what are you afraid of?
3. What are you feeling? What are you thinking about? What are your emotions?
4. On this occasion, what effect will your controlling have on others?
5. What would happen if others were left to take control themselves? How capable are they?
6. What could you do to make the situation successful without taking control?

Part
3

The mind: healthy attitudes

Activity: Where are you on the control scale?

You cannot do it all – but letting go of control can be scary. Control is not all or nothing, though.

You don't have to pass over full authority to someone when they lack the skills or confidence. It's about deciding how much to relinquish on this occasion – you can increase their level of freedom over time, as they develop and you become more trusting.

The degree of control you give them is based on a continuum. At one end is remaining directive and expecting the other people to carry out your instructions to the letter. At the other is fully empowering them to act in the way they decide.

1. Review the previous exercise, 'What do you have to have control over?' and choose an activity from question 4: something you take control over which someone else could do.
2. Who is involved?
3. Allocate a level of 'freedom' you will allow this person/group of people to have, and tick the box.

Activity
Person

Level	What you will allow the other party/parties to do	Tick
Level 7	Decide for themselves, take action, and no reporting necessary	
Level 6	Decide for themselves, take action, and only report if unsuccessful	
Level 5	Decide for themselves, take action, and report back to you when completed	
Level 4	Decide for themselves, take action, but regularly report back to you	
Level 3	Decide for themselves, but seek your approval before taking action their way	
Level 2	They make suggestions then you decide together how to act	
Level 1	You direct them on what action is to be taken and how	

4. How could you guide and support them to take on more authority themselves?

Top tips for Control Freaks

- **Be sensitive.** Become more sensitive to the needs of others. If they're asking for more responsibility but you're not allowing it, then it may be a sign that you're micromanaging.

- **Grow your awareness.** Practice noticing when you're becoming more controlling. Ask yourself how you would feel if you were being treated this way.

- **Reflect.** Regularly reflect on what you could do to be less controlling.

Part
3

The mind: healthy attitudes

- **Use an observer.** Ask a trusted ally to flag up to you when you go into control mode. Consider what triggered the need to control and what you could do to prevent the situation from occurring again.

- **Delegate effectively.** When you allow someone else to take control, you need to do this in a way that is influential and developmental, not bossy or dictatorial. Ensure that the other person understands:

  - Why the work needs to be done by them, not you
  - What the desired outcome is and how you will evaluate results
  - The date by which they are expected to do it
  - The resources and help they will have, to complete the work
  - The authority they have to make decisions
  - The problems they must refer back
  - How and when they should report to you on progress
  - How you propose to guide and support them

Activity: Your reflections

What has resonated with you while reading about the Control freak attitude?

- What have you learnt about yourself?
- What do you need to change?
- What do you need to start doing that you have not done before?
- What other thoughts do you have?

Part
3

The mind: healthy attitudes

11: Negative Thinker

- – Do you think it's safer to be more pessimistic than optimistic?
- – Do you focus more on the things that can and have gone wrong?
- – Do you find it difficult to see the funny side of life?
- – Do you focus more on what's bad in your job than good?
- – Do you assume things are hopeless first before even trying?
- – Do you often think about difficulties, failure and disasters?
- – Do you blow things out of proportion by thinking the worst?

If you answered Yes to any of these questions, you could be a Negative Thinker.

Case study

Yasmine had been in a meeting and was shocked at the end when one of her colleagues called her into a room and said, "Well, what would you suggest then? For some reason, you seem to find it easier to find the problems and to point out all the issues rather than offer any solutions. I feel we never make any progress".

Yasmin did have concerns when things were being changed. She didn't like taking risks and this made her worry. In fact, her worrying had gone up a notch to feeling anxious and this was affecting her ability to sleep.

She had a new manager who wanted to diversify the company's market offering and she found it hard to understand why he was being so free and easy with changing the way things were done. Clients wouldn't trust them anymore; they would lose their core business and their reputation. Change was too risky.

Yasmine was so wrapped up finding fault with everything that she failed to see the bigger picture and opportunities. She didn't register that if the company was going to survive and grow, it had to change.

This negative thinking was making Yasmine ill, but it didn't need to. Anxiety and feeling low are a sign of chronic stress. She needed to change her mindset. Pointing out potential pitfalls is a necessary part of planning for change, but it cannot overtake and prevent it. Yasmine would have been kinder to herself and reduced her anxiety if she had suggested solutions such as setting up a pilot scheme to test out the changes.

What is a Negative Thinker?

A Negative Thinker attitude is a subconscious, irrational thought-process where you look to the bad and discount the good. As Winston Churchill said, "The pessimist sees difficulty in every opportunity. The optimist sees the opportunity in every difficulty".

This creates a distorted version of reality, not caused by the situation itself but by the interpretation put on it by established personal beliefs, emotions (particularly fear) and internal standards. It is generally more prevalent than positive thinking primarily because it forms part of personal survival skills, alerting us to the possibility of danger and stimulating our imagination.

Your thoughts have a powerful effect on you, and a Negative Thinker attitude can best be described as a physiological toxin. It not only affects you mentally, but also physically. By creating anxiety and fear, it stimulates the stress response but also weakens the immune system, so people who maintain a negative attitude have more viral infections. This is because the cells that convey emotions to the brain are also present in your immune system.

How can being a Negative Thinker burn you out?

When you think positively, you feel in control, confident and happy to get on with life. This is recharging and energising – so much better than fear and anxiety. If you are going to prevent burnout, it is of great importance to transform your negative thoughts to positive ones.

With effort, conscious awareness and taking charge of your reactions, you can do so. Only you can do it, though, as you own your attitudes. By consciously evaluating the situation before you, you have the capability to take control of your thoughts and attitudes, and put yourself in charge.

Thoughts are always popping up in our minds. We can't stop them and we can't empty our minds, but we can challenge our thinking patterns, control our thoughts and retrain ourselves to make these more positive than negative. It's a question of rewiring the neurones to follow a different path which, if practiced frequently enough, will become the 'go-to' option.

Part
3

The mind: healthy attitudes

Activity: Your negative thoughts

1. Take a piece of paper and divide it into two columns. For three days, record in the left-hand column, all the negative opinions you express, aloud and inwardly, about your external world.
2. Count up how many negative thoughts you had each day.
3. At the end of three days, identify the themes that are emerging about the type of negative thoughts you have had.
4. In the right-hand column, reframe each negative thought to a positive one.

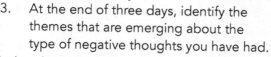

Activity: How did you come to that conclusion?

Attitudes are pretty settled ways of thinking about a situation or someone. They are formed from a person's values and their belief that something exists or is true ('if this, then that'). Beliefs are deeply set in the subconscious.

Since your attitude is influenced by your beliefs, the subconscious is a good place to start to identify what may underpin your negative thinking.

You can begin this by asking yourself a series of questions which will help you to identify where your beliefs may be distorting the reality of the situation. We call these 'Limiting Beliefs'.

The ABCD model provides a useful framework to explain this process.
- A = Adversity (a difficult or unpleasant situation)
- B = Belief (where you are confident that something exists or is true)
- C = Consequences (the emotional or behavioural result which is likely to be unpleasant)
- D = Determine the positive (the positive reality)

How it can go wrong: A - C thinking

An event takes place (A). When you use your subconscious mind to form an attitude, it has a powerful influence on your emotions and then how you feel and act (C).

Using only your subconscious mind means you operate A to C thinking. This means you go from A (the situation) straight to C (the action), missing out the part where you make sense of the situation. That's because you haven't engaged your conscious, rational thinking cerebral cortex.

How A-B-C thinking is better

If you want to change negative thinking to positive thinking, then you need to follow 'ABC' thinking instead. This means coming off autopilot and activating your conscious mindset between A and C.

This is 'B', where you evaluate the event and identify the underlying beliefs you hold about 'A'.

When you are aware of these, you are able to reflect on changing your viewpoint. When you go from A to B then to C, you are taking responsibility for your eventual response which will change 'C', the consequences.

If you want to develop resilience, then you need to develop B-C thinking. This means reviewing your beliefs and taking control of the way you will subsequently act. It is not about dwelling for any length of time on what happened in A or how you feel in C, but directing your focus to why you feel this way. What do you believe to be true? Is it actually the case? What would be a healthier belief, that would prevent you triggering the stress response?

Step 1: **A = Activating event** Recall a situation when you had a negative thought	
Step 2: **C = Consequences** What were the consequences and how did it make you feel?	
Step 3: B = Beliefs 1. What do you believe to be true that led to this negative thinking? 2. Why do you have this belief?	

3. How realistic is it and what is the proof?
- What do you have as evidence?
- Is it observed or based on hearsay?
- Did you make any assumptions?
- Have you ignored any information?
- What positives are you ignoring?

4. What effect did it have on you and the outcome?

5. What did you miss out on by having this belief?

6. How might someone else have viewed the situation?

7. How would you feel if someone else was expressing these negative thoughts?

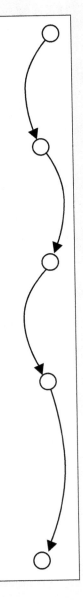

Step 4: **D = Determine the positive** 1. Identify a new positive belief about the situation 2. Why would this be better for you?	

Top tips for reframing negative thoughts to positive thoughts:

- **Start each morning positively.** Make your first thought each morning a positive one!

- **Break the cycle.** The more you think negative thoughts, the more embedded they will become, so it is important to break the cycle. Use questions to clarify the meaning of your attitudes, to establish where you are limiting the reality, and to identify what choices you have.

- **Be calm.** You need to be focused on the present (not the past or the future) and develop a clear, calm persona that will enable you to think more positively and with greater perspective about what's going on around you.

- **Take a breath.** Calm the mind to engage the cortex and use this for logical reasoning. Take three long deep breaths or think about something that makes you feel calm and happy – examples may be the cat curled up by you or maybe a beautiful cherry tree in full blossom.

- **Check-in with yourself.** Self-awareness is so important. Make an effort to regularly check-in with your thoughts. Are they positive or negative? Spend time reviewing the negative thoughts. How much are they taking over/absorbing your thinking capacity right now? If it's too much, you need to switch your thinking to the positive aspect of the situation. The ideal ratio is four positive thoughts for every one negative thought.

- **See the possibilities** not the limitations.

- **Be solution-focused** not problem-orientated.

Activity: Your new best friend

1. Imagine someone you know who is positive and confident.

    a. What do they look like?
    b. What do they say?
    c. How do they behave?

2. Now imagine yourself stepping inside them. Become every part of them, how they talk and behave. What does it feel like being around them?

3. How will you become them? What can you change in yourself to become them?

Person	Positive attributes and behaviours	How can I become them?

Part
3

The mind: healthy attitudes

Activity: Your reflections

What has resonated with you while reading about the Negative Thinker attitude?

- What have you learnt about yourself?
- What do you need to change?
- What do you need to start doing that you have not done before?
- What other thoughts do you have?

12: Inner Critic

- Do you have a voice inside your head always on alert to critique or judge you?
- When you've made a mistake, do you find it hard to switch off the internal chatter?
- Do you blame yourself when something fails, even if it's a team effort?
- Do you place more emphasis on your weaknesses than your strengths?
- Do you have a tendency to think people don't like you?
- Do you feel worthless?

If you answered Yes to any of these questions, you could be an Inner Critic.

Case study

Jess had been offered the opportunity to work on an interesting project and the more she thought about it, the less likely she was to accept it. Her mind had gone into overdrive. It was like having someone living in her head constantly talking at her.

This inner chatter meant she couldn't stop churning thoughts over in her head and weighing up how able she was. 'Why have they chosen you? You're not up to it. You're much more likely to make a mess of it.' She felt that taking on this project would expose her and then she'd get blamed when it all went wrong.

In the course of twenty-four hours, Jess had convinced herself that she was not up to it. She doubted her capability and the only way to clear her head and calm herself was to tell the company that she wasn't the best person and to choose someone else.

Jess's inner critic had made her believe that she was not up to it and would end up exposed as a fraud – something we call 'Imposter Syndrome'.

The reality is that she wouldn't have been asked to take this role on if she was a fraud. By allowing her inner critic to take over, Jess let it rob her of the opportunity to develop her skills further and left her riddled with self-doubt. This means she won't feel up to taking on anything developmental in the future and her career could stagnate. Taking on something new is not easy, but achieving success does improve self-confidence and self-esteem.

What is an Inner Critic?

Inner Critic is the voice inside your head that judges and criticises you. Instead of allowing you to reflect on a mistake or poor outcome and directing you to how you can improve, this self-talk generates negative attitudes about yourself that leave you feeling that you're not good enough, dampening your mood and emotions.

How can being an Inner Critic burn you out?

If allowed to dominate to the extent that we discount the positive and amplify the negative about ourselves, it becomes a form of self-sabotage that significantly impacts our self-esteem and self-confidence – after all, if you keep saying you can't do something, you won't be able to. Left unchecked, the Inner Critic will sabotage performance, relationships, happiness and joy of life.

That's why it's important to control it. Why beat yourself up and allow it to ruin your life if you're not in danger? To control your Inner Critic, you need to take control of your self-talk and put a stop to the sabotaging thoughts and emotions it stirs up.

Activity: What is the true value of your Inner Critic chatter?

Self-esteem is your emotional opinion about yourself which protects you from the hurtful comments of others. An Inner Critic mindset has a big, negative impact on our self-esteem. That's why it's important that you become more aware of what this demon in your head is telling you and whether it is really necessary to be so hard on yourself.

1. For the next week, write down everything your Inner Critic is telling you. Do this in the second person, 'You are...'. Rather than in the first person, 'I am...'.

2. Then ask yourself the following:

    a. How valuable is this advice? What is it trying to achieve? Will it protect you from harm or not?
    b. What triggers your Inner Critic? (For example, a criticism from someone else, tiredness, fear)
    c. What aspects of your life is it judging? For example, work, body image, capability.
    d. How does it make you feel physically, mentally and emotionally?

3. At the end of the week, review everything you have written down.

    a. Which judgements have had the greatest negative effect on you?
    b. How justified were they? What is the reality?

c. These negative judgements are called self-limiting beliefs. How have they limited you?

4. Review the judgements that have had the greatest negative effect on you and find a new perspective that is more positive and kinder to you. This doesn't mean you change the statement to be a positive one, because this may not reflect the reality or provide you with something to learn from. Look to find one that isn't as critical and distressing.

   This may be something along the lines of changing: "You are so stupid, making that simple spelling mistake", to: "You made a mistake. Luckily it was only one... and it's incredibly hard to produce such a lengthy document with no mistakes".

5. Repeat this exercise regularly. It's not easy and it takes time, but it's important that you become more aware of what your Inner Critic is telling you, how this is harming you, and how you can become kinder to yourself.

Activity: Who is your Inner Critic?

While the Inner Critic works away subconsciously, it's part of you. It's important to identify and separate the Inner Critic from who you really are. Don't allow it to take over and destroy you.

1. Create a picture of who your Inner Critic is.
   a. What is its persona?
   b. What does it look like?
   c. What sort of voice does it have?
   d. How does it talk – tone, speed, accent? Is it rational, scared, angry, belittling?

2. Now imagine your Inner Critic as someone gentler and supportive or even someone who causes amusement when it kicks off, like a cartoon character.
   a. Draw or find a picture to represent it.
   b. Give your Inner Critic a name.

3. Distance yourself from this character. When it starts, tell it firmly that you have no time for it today, so stop.

Part

3

The mind: healthy attitudes

Activity: Your brand

You can use this exercise when your Inner Critic goes too far and is dominating your thinking.

The aim of the exercise is to remind yourself how special you really are - and you **are** special!

Consider your skills, knowledge, experience (education, work, travel, overcoming challenges, volunteering), people skills, hobbies and interests, achievements – anything and everything that makes you unique and special.

Write it all down in the box below. Then photocopy the page and put it in your desk at work, on the back of your wardrobe door, on a kitchen cupboard – anywhere where you will see it.

Top tips to remove the Inner Critic from your thoughts:

- **Positive self-talk.** Every morning and evening look yourself in the eye in the mirror and tell yourself how wonderful you are. You are awesome! Pick something that has gone really well that day... for example: "You are a fantastic report writer". Say it with conviction, otherwise you won't believe it.

- **Positive affirmations.** Have a variety of short, punchy, powerful statements about yourself beginning with "I am...". These are called affirmations. They build confidence and self-respect and fire up happy chemicals in the brain. Affirmations must be in the present and positive. I am courageous, I am important, I am confident, I am patient, I am forgiving, I am beautiful/handsome, I am optimistic, I am bright and intelligent, I am talented. These are all examples. Repeat at regular times during the day.

- **Seek feedback.** Ask someone you love or respect to tell you what you do well. Don't ask about the negatives. Just take the positives and think about them. Why is this the case? What skills, abilities and mental talents enable this? This is a great way to boost your self-esteem.

- **Use a coach.** Have a work or life coach to work on building your confidence. The stronger your confidence, the quieter your Inner Critic's voice will become.

- **Mirror others.** Identify the qualities you admire in others. If you see them in others, it's likely that you have them yourself – they just might be buried under negative thinking.

- **Keep a diary.** Each day, record three things that you have done well that day. Add pictures and sayings so that when you feel bad, you can look at your diary and allow the positive feelings to envelop you.

- **Practice positive behaviours.** Ideas include smiling at people, mixing with positive people, celebrating success and achievements.

- **Take exercise.** Make time to be active and exercise. Exercise triggers endorphins which make you feel good and aid positivity.

Part
3

The mind: healthy attitudes

- **Study mindfulness.** Practice daily. This will train you to reduce the chatter by moving the mind away from reliving the past or worrying about the future, to focusing on the here and now.

- **Share your thoughts.** Share with a trusted friend, colleague or family member. Ask them to be honest; it won't do you any good if they just tell you not to worry.

- **Socialise.** Don't lock yourself away with your negative thoughts – meet up with people.

- **Clear those negative thoughts.** Take a deep breath and at the same time imagine wrapping your thoughts up in a piece of paper. As you breathe out, throw the paper in the bin.

- **Take professional help.** If your Inner Critic is really sabotaging you, consider seeing a cognitive behavioural therapy (CBT) coach who will help you to see that the thoughts you hold may be self-defeating and how you can counter them with more positive thoughts.

Activity: Your reflections

What has resonated with you while reading about the Inner Critic attitude?

- What have you learnt about yourself?
- What do you need to change?
- What do you need to start doing that you have not done before?
- What other thoughts do you have?

13: Social Isolator

- Do you believe that you get more done by being on your own?
- Do you prefer not to talk or engage with colleagues in case they expect something from you?
- Are you so focused on your work that you have little time for socialising right now?
- Do you find you have no time for interests and hobbies outside of work right now?
- Do you find people an unnecessary distraction right now?
- Do you lack the energy to listen to someone else's problems right now?
- Are people telling you they haven't seen much of you lately?

If you answered Yes to any of these questions, you could be a Social Isolator.

Case study

Ali was an accountant. Although his workload tended to go in cycles, year-end being particularly busy, his activities were actually increasing in complexity and volume across the year. It was becoming more of a struggle to keep on top of it, but this was a great firm to be working for and he had his eyes on being a partner one day, so he just needed to focus more, and deliver.

The firm had a culture of socialising together. They'd regularly meet up after work for a drink or meal. He felt he didn't have time for this. If he was going to get on top of things, the best solution to freeing up some extra time was to not go to the after work meet-ups. He did this a couple of times and the quietness of the office at that time in the evening meant he got quite a bit done.

The longer time went on, the more Ali pulled back on socialising and replacing it with working. In time, he even started cancelling on friends and family as well.

At his annual performance review, he expected his manager to give him a glowing report and recommend a bonus – after all, he was working exceptionally hard. To his shock and surprise, his manager questioned his commitment to the company! How dare he, when he was on the verge of collapse from working every waking hour?

The review turned out to be a wake-up call – now he could recognise just how exhausted he was. He'd fall asleep on the train going home, grab something easy to cook at the station, gobble it down once back at home then crawl into bed, only to wake abruptly in the night in a sweat, with his heart thumping, and so the day started all over again.

Ali might have been working harder and harder, but the way he was doing it showed he was addicted and losing sight of reality. His company questioned his commitment because he was not being seen. Their determinant of success – which is true for many companies – was as much about being part of the social scene as doing the work.

Ali had the balance all wrong and paid the price, not only financially but also with his health, because his adrenals were being overworked as he was struggling to cope.

What is a Social Isolator?

Social Isolator is an attitude that says you need to separate yourself from others for the time being.

As humans, we thrive best when we connect with others. The giving and receiving of attention and love feeds our reward system and makes us feel stronger, happier and more resilient. Although being alone can be helpful for reflection and recovery, it is only beneficial when it is a for a short time. Prolonged social isolation, with no beneficial gain, is physically, mentally and emotionally harmful. It triggers negative thoughts, emotions and feelings so that the more you isolate yourself, the more anxious, depressed and low you will feel.

How can being a Social Isolator burn you out?

A Social Isolator risks burnout because when isolated, we lose our sense of time, which is why we end up working harder and isolating ourselves more. Our ability to benchmark ourselves against others goes, diminishing our self-confidence and self-esteem.

Isolation may arise from being naturally self-contained, preferring your own company or because you have so many demands to contend with that you believe that it's best, for the time being, to be alone and just get on with it, with as few distractions as possible. In other words, it's a sign of stress!

Part

3

The mind: healthy attitudes

Activity: Your isolationist tendencies

As humans we thrive best when connected with others.

1. Why do you have a Social Isolation attitude right now?
2. What are you trying to achieve by being alone?
3. Is this healthy?
4. How is it making you feel?
5. What are your family, friends and colleagues telling you? For example: "Where have you been? I haven't seen you for ages".

Activity: Important relationships

Some relationships energise us, while others drain our energy. To prevent burnout, it is important to make time for the relationships that energise you, make you feel good and feed your happiness.

1. Identify the important relationships in your life – personal and professional.

2. Consider first, the relationships that energise you:
   a. How often do you see each person?
   b. What do you gain from the time you spend with each person?
   c. What can you do to see more of each person?

3. Identify the relationships that drain your energy.
   a. How often do you see each person?
   b. What do you lose from the time you spend with each person?
   c. What can you do to see less of each person? Can you find a way to manage the relationships to become more positive?

Top tips to become more connected

Look at the list below. What actions could you take to prevent you from isolating yourself?

- **Start a new hobby.** If you're finding work colleagues are too much for you right now, take up a hobby. This will provide social contact without too much connection: maybe a new sport or taking up a craft?

- **Volunteer.** Being kind to someone stimulates dopamine and serotonin, two chemicals in the brain associated with feeling good. Being kind to others provides a sense of reward and happiness which you may be struggling to get at work.

- **Connect with people.** Smile at anyone who comes within two metres of you. If they smile back, you will feel connected inside.

- **Walk a dog.** This can be very sociable as dog walkers love to chat, particularly if the dog is cute! Walking also reduces elevated cortisol, which will help your adrenals.

- **Use your diary.** Schedule time in your diary to speak to friends. If you're finding it hard to meet up, this at least keeps the connection going.

- **Talk to a counsellor or help line.** Find out if your company contracts to an Employee Assistance Provider (EAP). This is a confidential service that provides the facility to talk about anything from financial worries, child care problems and health issues. If not, try your GP or the Samaritans or Google for counselling services in your area.

- **Don't bottle things up.** Speak to close friends or family who have more experience. Share worries and concerns and work with them to put the situation into perspective. This can be liberating. Just talking through your issues can help you put them in perspective and improve your attitudes and mood.

- **Ask for help and support when you need it.** It is not a sign of weakness or ineptitude.

Part

3

The mind: healthy attitudes

Activity: Your reflections

What has resonated with you while reading about the Social Isolator attitude?

- What have you learnt about yourself?
- What do you need to change?
- What do you need to start doing that you have not done before?
- What other thoughts do you have?

14: People Pleaser

- Do you find it almost impossible to say 'No' to someone's request?
- Do you feel guilty when you say 'No', so end up giving in?
- Do you find it hard to be assertive?
- Do you feel obliged to help people more senior to you, no matter how busy you are?
- Do you feel put-upon because people are abusing your generosity?

If you answered Yes to any of these questions, you could be a People Pleaser.

Case study

Sophie taught history in a secondary school. Most of her classes covered exam courses. The previous year she had a pupil who asked if she would mark an extra essay she had written. Sophie was delighted that the pupil had taken the initiative and willingly did it.

When the pupil moved on to studying A Levels, she asked again but at this level, each essay required more analysis and feedback. The pupil must have shared this opportunity with others, because other pupils submitted extra essays, asking for analysis and feedback.

Sophie was annoyed with herself that she'd said yes and hadn't made it more public in class that the work they are set will give them enough practice to do well in the exam. She felt she couldn't say no now as she'd be letting the pupils down and she didn't want her pupils to dislike her as a teacher.

As well as essays, the pupils then began to request Sophie's time during the lunch hour to explain elements of the work covered in class that morning. Sophie found that she had no free time and was struggling to keep up with her usual work. She began to come into the school an hour earlier and stay later to keep on top of marking and preparation.

Sophie became exhausted. Her hair was falling out, she was gaining weight, but worst of all, her mind was becoming foggy and she was struggling to concentrate and remember things. She was thankful that it was close to the end of term. By the end of term Sophie hardly had the energy to make a cup of tea. She eventually went to see her doctor who did some blood tests. The result was Sophie had developed an autoimmune condition of her thyroid gland.

Not saying no was founded on fear - the fear of not being liked. Feeling extra pressure from the pupils to take more on left Sophie feeling out of control. Feeling out of control triggers the HPA-axis. This incessant cascade of stress hormones compromised Sophie's immune system in a way that began to target her thyroid gland, killing off cells and leaving her no longer able to produce enough thyroid hormone. This is a condition that requires medication for life.

There's a saying: 'your biography becomes your biology' and in Sophie's case this couldn't have been more true. Work, or as I should really say, 'failing to say no', had made her ill.

What is a People Pleaser?

People Pleasers have an attitude that they cannot say 'No' to a request from someone else because of what they believe the consequences will be. It's the same even when they do not have the capacity to fulfil this demand.

How can being a People Pleaser burn you out?

These self-fabricated consequences are rarely grounded in fact. It could be that they have a belief that saying 'No' will make the other person angry enough to put the relationship at risk. If the other party is someone more senior, then they may feel obliged to agree, fearing that saying 'No' will put their career at risk. Or maybe it's because the feeling of guilt is just too unpleasant to bear.

The ironic thing is that absorbing these extra demands puts People Pleasers in a position of risking burnout. If this happens, relationships become strained, their careers stall and the feelings of helplessness and despair are far worse than a momentary feeling of guilt.

To prevent burnout, it is vitally important to recognise when this 'kindness' is really about pleasing people at your own expense. It means putting yourself in control of the situation by focusing on YOUR priorities - the important things you need to achieve. To enable this, you need to be aware of how the other party's request fits with your circumstances, capabilities and commitments and then feel empowered to deal with it in a way that doesn't leave you feeling frustrated and imposed upon, or worried and guilty. In other words, it's about listening to, and acting on, your inner voice.

Part 3

The mind: healthy attitudes

Activity: Why is saying 'No' such a problem for you?

You are entitled to make choices, so why is it so difficult for you to say 'No'? To find the underlying reasons, work your way through the following questions:

1. Who do you find it difficult to say 'No' to?
2. How would saying 'No' to this person make you feel?
3. Why do you have this attitude – what are you telling yourself? What do you consider the consequences will be?
4. What evidence do you have that the consequences will be as you imagine?
5. What would happen if you said 'No'?
6. What choices do you have?

Remember, you have nothing to feel guilty about if you have a justified reason. In many cases, the other party respects someone who can stand up for themselves.

Activity: What are your boundaries?

It is important that you know your limits and have rules and boundaries which you can use to justify your decision to decline to help.

Complete the following chart:

What will I say Yes to? Why?	What can I say No to? Why?

The mind: healthy attitudes

Activity: Saying 'No'

The key is to learn to say 'No' without feeling guilty. You have a right to say 'No' and not feel bad about it, but it takes practice to build the confidence to do this. Begin at home, and practice what you could say.

1. Choose something you would normally say 'Yes' to and instead of saying 'Yes', say 'No.' It doesn't need to be something major – initially, the simpler the better. It is important that you resist all efforts to change your mind and stick by your conviction. Continue this for one day.

2. The following day, choose something else and continue this process for up to seven days.

3. Keep a diary:
   a. What did you say 'No' to?
   b. How did you say 'No' and what response did you receive?
   c. How did this make you feel?
   d. What was your body language like? Did you stand up straight and look sincere or did you smile and look apologetic, weakening your case.
   e. What was your tone like?
   f. Why should you NOT feel guilty?

4. At the end of the process, review how your feelings have changed.

Remember: saying 'No' in this way allows you to say 'Yes' to the things you really want to do – the things that will energise and motivate you and prevent burnout.

It might not be a question of saying 'No' outright. It may be a 'No' right now, but a 'Yes' later. Or it may be a 'No' for you on your own, but a 'Yes' if someone else was involved to help you, or more information was provided.

Top tips for saying 'No':

- **Be more proactive.** Discuss commitments and deadlines with your manager so when they ask you to drop everything, you can remind them why it is not possible.

- **State your position.** It's not about just saying 'No'. Offering a statement that sets out your position softens your response. "I'm afraid I can't right now – I have a major deadline to meet by 4pm tomorrow".

- **Have words up your sleeve** that you can use when you initially respond. Be firm, but empathic: "I'm afraid that's not possible", "I'm afraid there's no chance right now", "I'd rather not because…", "I'm not the right person to ask right now…"

- **Take control of the situation.** Stand up, if they're standing. Listen, think, respond. Do not feel obliged to ask any questions; it may weaken your response. If you have an inkling that they're going to ask you to do something, pre-empt them and say, "I have a suspicion that you're going to ask me to do something for you. I'm sorry, but it's absolutely out of the question right now".

- **Keep a record.** If it's hard to say 'No' and you frequently have to capitulate, then keep a record of the extras being asked and the impact this has on your workload and your capacity to cope. Have a conversation with that person about the impact they are having on your workload and set some expectations on how to better manage this going forward.

Part

3

The mind: healthy attitudes

Activity: Assertive message

Saying 'No' requires you to be assertive. Assertiveness is about getting your point across confidently and without aggression.

Try this three-step framework to structure your conversation. Rehearse it in the mirror four times to build your confidence.

1. What is the situation? Why is this a problem?
2. **Step one:** acknowledge what the requestor has said: "I appreciate that your client needs this by the end of the day".
3. Use a **'link word'**: then say, 'however' or 'on the other hand'. Do not say 'but' as this is perceived as becoming aggressive.
4. **Step two:** state what you think or feel: "However, I'm about to go into a long meeting with one of my clients and will then have a considerable amount of follow-up work to do".
5. **Link word:** You are about to make a suggestion, so say "...and..."
6. **Step three:** "...and would welcome some time with you to discuss the outcomes".

Eye contact is really important when being assertive. Looking away gives the impression that you are uncertain, so when giving your message, make good eye contact. Make sure your posture projects confidence – stand or sit upright but relax your arms and be conscious of the space between you both. Too close is intimidating; too far away loses power.

Activity: Your reflections

What has resonated with you while reading about the People Pleaser attitude?

- What have you learnt about yourself?
- What do you need to change?
- What do you need to start doing that you have not done before?
- What other thoughts do you have?

Part 4
The way forward

15: My action plan to prevent burnout

Activity: My action plan to prevent burnout

Review the book and the answers to the exercises you have completed. What are you going to do to prevent burnout?

Preventing burnout is about healthy adrenals and healthy attitudes.

1. Overall, what have you learnt from reading this book?

Review each of the Your Reflection activities you have completed as you have worked your way through the book.

Healthy Adrenals	Healthy Attitudes

2. What will you do to optimise your adrenal function?

3. What will you do to create healthy attitudes?

Which of the seven attitudes described in this book are increasing your risk of burnout?

What changes will you make to change these attitudes? Address each attitude in turn.

What do you need to take responsibility for and where do you need to involve others?

How will you ensure you don't slip back into your old ways?

Part

4

The way forward

It is important that you are able to sustain the actions you have committed to. To aid this, it can be helpful to know what you want from life. You can only achieve this, and enjoy the outcome, if you have mental and physical wellbeing.

Whenever you feel you may be slipping back into your old ways, read this section. This is what your life is about.

4. **If I could wave a magic wand, what would your life be like?**

16: And to support you...

I hope you have enjoyed this book and found it of immense value to you and your wellbeing.

Perhaps at times it has challenged you, but driving a career and ensuring that it's not at the expense of your health is challenging by its very nature.

Overcoming challenges takes us out of our comfort zone and opens up a whole new world to us. It ignites our capacity to grow and become more resilient and successful.

With such a vast topic, there is only so much room for explanation. If you require any further information or tips on how to propel your career, then go to our website at **www.youngprofs.net**

Let us know how you get on. Your stories of transformation are always of great interest to me. It's real people that bring this topic alive, and I for one am still learning.

You can reach me on **susan@youngprofs.net**

We also have two other books in the series:

- **How to have an outstanding career**
- **The Young Professional's Guide to optimising your personal energy**

Both are practical guides that contain lots of theory and many more exercises that you will not find in this book. Go to our website for further information.

To finish, here are some top tips for preventing burnout. Despite the madness of the ever-changing and volatile world we live and work in, we can still remain healthy by paying attention to and taking action over the following:

- Be mindful of your physical, mental and emotional being. Listen to what your body is telling you. Do you feel irritable, do your shoulders ache, do you feel dizzy standing up? If yes, what can you do about it?

- Identify the source of your stress and address it as a priority. If that's difficult, keep a stress diary.

- Good food can build resilience so eat well and regularly. Eat foods that build your strength and resilience such as good quality protein, wholegrains and vegetables, and keep well hydrated with water.

- Balance your blood sugar. If you don't, cortisol will be taking on this role, adding yet something else to burn you out. Eat healthy, slow energy-releasing foods regularly. If you plan meals in advance, you'll be able to bring food into work.

- Eat gut-friendly foods that boost your good bacteria. Bacteria suffers when you're stuck in 'always-on'. Feed the good bacteria you have with onions, leeks and chicory and take more in with natural live yoghurt, kefir, kimchi and sauerkraut.

- Take care with stimulants such as coffee, alcohol and cigarettes. Stimulants trigger cortisol, putting an extra strain on your adrenals and alter your sleep cycle, increasing the burden on your adrenals even further. If addicted, come off them very slowly, otherwise you'll get a headache.

- If you're struggling to cope, consider taking some supplements to provide extra nutrients to support your stress response. Vitamin B, particularly B5, and vitamin C will be in high demand for the production of adrenal hormones.

- Exercise. It uses up excess glucose in the bloodstream helping to balance your blood sugars. Make sure the exercise is appropriate for the health of your adrenals as exercise raises cortisol.

- Take time out at lunch time and do something uplifting to clear your mind and raise your energy, such as a walk or meeting someone who makes you laugh.

- Take regular breaks from intense work – our body clock works in cycles and regularly seeks recovery time. Break each hour into 50 minutes of focused activity followed by a 10-minute break.

- Manage digital technology – don't let it take over and manage you.

- Do everything you can to get a good night's sleep. Just one broken night triggers the stress response.

- Take the time to check in with who you are. How do you respond to stress, what are the triggers, how could you behave in a different way to ensure you don't trigger a stress response in yourself and others? You not only have a responsibility to look after your wellbeing but you also have a duty to make sure your behaviour doesn't trigger stress in anyone else.

Part

4

The way forward

- Ask yourself: does it have to be perfect? Life isn't perfect, so what would happen if you didn't submit this work absolutely perfectly? Give yourself permission to make a mistake.

- Write a to-do list for the next day and prioritise your activities. Start the day with the most important task – not your emails.

- Look for possibilities, not limitations.

- Learn to say 'No'. You don't have to say yes to anything you do not have the capacity to fulfil.

- Identify your priorities in life; family, work, sport, pets. Prepare strategies for how you will embrace these with balance in your life.

- Have fun and laugh. It's the best medicine.

- Welcome the support and friendship of your family and friends and make time for them, particularly if you are starting to isolate yourself.

- If you need it, get help. Things can't always be solved alone. It is nothing to be ashamed of. You are in this situation because of how hard you work.

And above all...

...be kind to yourself.

Part
4

The way forward

Lightning Source UK Ltd.
Milton Keynes UK
UKOW06f0936160917
309288UK00006B/249/P